ESCAPING THE DARKNESS
RUNNING FROM MY DREAMS

Christopher Bice

www.darkmythproductions.com/publications

> The sale of this book without its cover is unauthorized. If you purchased this book without a cover, you should be aware that it was reported to the publisher as "unsold and destroyed." Neither the author nor the publisher has received payment for the sale of this "stripped book."

This book is a work of fiction. Names, characters, places, and incidents are products of the author's imagination or are used fictitiously. Any resemblance to actual events or locales or persons, living or dead, is entirely coincidental.

Dark Myth Publications, a division of
The JayZoMon/Dark Myth Company.
21050 Little Beaver Rd, Apple Valley, CA 92308

Copyright 2021 by Christopher Bice

All rights reserved, including the right to reproduce this book or portions thereof in any form whatsoever.
For information address, 21050 Little Beaver Rd, Apple Valley, Ca 92308

ISBN: 978-1-7372947-1-9

First Printing June 2021

Dark Myth Publications is a registered trademark of The JayZoMon/Dark Myth Company

10 9 8 7 6 5 4 3 2 1

Table of Contents

LOVE

Again & Again..3
Best Friend..4
Broken Heart...5
Chrysanthemum...6
Daughters..7
Daydream..8
De Ja Vu..9
Desert Love...10
Dreams Of You...11
Eternal Kiss...12
Eternal Love...13
Eternally Yours...14
First Kiss...15
Forbidden Places...16
Freight Train Blues..17
Goodbye To Love..18
Harvest Moon..19
I Am Here...20
I Remember You..21
In My Dreams..22
In My Thoughts...23
Letter Home...24
Lost Love..25
Lost Season..26
Love...27
Love's Perils...28

Table of Contents (Cont'd)

Love's Quest 29
Making Memories 30
Moving On 31
My Desert 32
My Regrets 33
Passions 34
Secret In My Heart 35
Shared Memories 36
Should I Go 37
Spring 38
Springtime 39
Stolen Heart 40
Teddy Bear 41
The Crescent Moon 43
The Dream 44
The Gift 45
The Jungle 46
The Lazy River 47
The Looking Glass 48
The Lovers 49
The Painting 50
The Sonnet 51
The Voyage 52
Time Moves On 53
Tinker Bell 54
Twilight Prayers 55
Vampire Love 56
Where Angels Walk 57
Winter's Rest 58
Wishes 59

Table of Contents (Cont'd)

Your Evil ways..60

DEATH

A Child's Remorse..63
A Promise..64
Always..65
Black Lake...66
Broken Lines...67
Catching A Cloud...68
Chiseled In Stone...69
Daddy...70
Death Of A Child...71
Dream...72
Electric Dreams..73
Going Home...74
Home Again..75
I'm Coming Home...77
Little White Lie...79
Masks..80
Missing You..81
Monsters..82
My Best Friend...83
The Closet...84
My Goodbye...85
New Day..86
Nuclear Wind...87
Saying Goodbye...88
Song Birds...89

Table of Contents (Cont'd)

The 5 W's..90
The Final Round..91
The Last Kiss...92
The Last Score...93
The Long Road Home...94
The Promise...95
The Taste Of Sorrow..96
The Tempest..97
Time..98
Wanted Dead Or Alive..99

INSPIRATION

Christmas Prayer...103
An Honest Man...105
Ballerina...106
Little Blue Pony...107
Choices...108
Daisies..109
Darkness...110
Desert Breath...111
Distant Drums...112
Doorway...113
Dragonfly...114
Easter Lily..115
Easter Poem...116
End Of Days..117
Every Day Is Mental Illness Day...118
Fishing Town..119

Table of Contents (Cont'd)

A Day In The Desert (Haikus)..120
Heaven Bound...121
I Am Merlin..122
Lady Of The Woods..124
Let's Talk..125
Lines..126
Listen...127
Mirage..128
Morning Prayer...129
My Friend..130
My Guide...131
My Happy Place...132
My Journey...133
New Beginnings...135
Petals..136
Pictures From My Mind...137
Please, Please, I Want To Stay..138
PoetsA...140
Prejudice...141
Rebirth..142
Regret..143
Repent...144
Ripples..145
Salvation...146
Saved...147
Searching..149
Second Chance..150
The Brook...152
The Cowboy...153
The Dolphin's Dance...154

Table of Contents (Cont'd)

The Door..155
The Fog...157
The Hitchhiker..158
The Mountain...159
The Painter...160
The Path..161
The Pear Tree..162
The Pool..163
The Quill..164
The Road To Salvation.......................................165
The Sands...166
The Story Teller..167
The Thief...169
The Veil...171
What Goals Do We Have As Modern Man.......172
Wordless...173
Words 1.0...174
Words 2.1...175
Words 3.16...176

MADNESS

Apocalypse..179
A Criminal Mind...181
A Stranger In Town..182
Betrayal...183
Birth...184
Destiny..185
Disposable Person..186

Table of Contents (Cont'd)

Dust 187
Extinction 188
Genocide 189
Hello 190
Hunter's Moon 191
Insanity 192
Killing My Demons 193
Lessons Learned 194
Lonely Street 195
Love's Feast 196
Lover's Kiss 197
Memories 198
Multiples 199
My Magic Phone 200
New Year 201
Pandemic 202
Retribution 203
Shattered 204
Shipwreck 205
Tears Of The Damned 206
The Banshee 207
The Birth Of Madness 209
The Book 210
The Breakdown 211
The Dungeon Master 212
The Evil Within 213
The Grim Reaper 215
The Madness 216
   The Scale 217
The Seventh Son 219

Table of Contents (Cont'd)

The Tower..220
The Wilderness..221
The Wizard..222
Unbelievers...223
Untitled Unfinished...224
Working Man..226

ABOUT THE POET

About the Poet..227

Dedications

For my wife Janet whose faith in me kept me moving forward.

ESCAPING THE DARKNESS
RUNNING FROM MY DREAMS

LOVE

Again & Again

I catch a glimpse of you

You live between worlds

A feeling of déjà vu

I've known you before

You were...no

You are a part of me

Through time and space

Different periods throughout

Landmarks call to me

A heart carved in a tree

A hint of perfume

Your auburn hair in sunlight

Sparking memories

Moments in time

I have inscribed you forever

In my heart and my mind

So I can live this moment

Again and again.

Best Friend

When first we met
I was alone and scared
Emotionally lost
Crying uncontrollably

You were there for me
You shared your love
Gave me purpose
Taught me independence

In return I gave you
My love and kisses
Warm snuggles at night
Something tangible to hold

As I grow emotionally
Mature into all I can be
One thing stands out clearly
You taught me to play!

Broken Heart

You stayed out until three a.m.
You wouldn't tell me where you'd been
I can't take this heartache anymore
This time I'm walking out the door

> We promised we'd always be true
> But cheating comes so easy for you
> I'll not listen to anymore lies
> Cause this time it's your turn to cry

There's a rundown motel in town
That's where my tears will come down
I just need a quiet place to get away
To pretend you'll love me another day

> Chorus

I can't take these lies anymore
I've heard them all many times before
My broken heart tells me to walk away
But my pride tells me don't give up this way

> Chorus

At least you know where I can be found
If your cheating heart wants to come around.
I'll dry my tears away
Maybe love will come one more day.

Chrysanthemum

As you glide across my face
Hundreds of silk petals
Tantalizing my chin
Exciting my senses

A body so slender
Raising your face to the sun
I smell your essence
Your sweet perfume

Beauty beyond compare
Gracefully you dance
In the warm summer breeze
You have hypnotized me

Your beauty captures me
I must process you
Nourish you, love you
Before death takes us both.

Daughters

I witnessed the sprout
Coming forth glistening
I watched as this hybrid
Matured to an exceptional beauty
A flowering daughter
With a velvety smoothness
Opening up to many layers
Whose soul emits beautiful fragrances
Of pure innocence

Then he came
Admiring her beauty
Breathing in her essence
Her fragrance exciting him
He must have her
Own her
Display her
He tries to pluck her
But she attacks

With razor thorns
Little knives
She frees herself
From he that would possess her
She's a splice from her
Mother
Strong of body
With sharp defensives
And she will bleed any
That try to control her.

Daydream

Our eyes meet from across the room
You bewitched me
Capturing my soul
I see us sneaking away
To suddenly embrace
Behind a locked door
Arms wrapped around you
My lips crushing yours
Our tongues exploring
My hands caress your curves
You rip buttons from my shirt
Low guttural moans
Your back against the wall
Nowhere to run
From the heat
From the moment
Sweat glistens
Basic animal needs
As passions reach a crescendo
My daydream ends
As you stroll past my table
A subtle wink from you
As one bead of sweat
Trails from your temple

De Ja Vu

I awaken from a restless sleep
A cold sweat envelops me
Again you have invaded my dreams
Feelings of déjà vu torment me
Who are you
From where do you come
I force myself to rise
Pushing you away
But you consume me
Are you my future
Perhaps deep within my past
My previous life
A different plane of existence
I can no longer control my passions
The heat rises within me
I must…know you
My soul cries out for you
If you are but a dream
Then Death take me
So I might lie forever
In your arms.

Desert Love

As I sit sipping my morning tea
Legs wrapped against the cold air
The birth of a new day
A promise of heat to come

My mind travels unconnected
Back to her
To my one true love
Again, my heart beats faster

I see her now in my mind
Lips as red as cactus flowers
Temper as sharp as its thorns
Eyes as green as emerald waters

I fell in love as she twirled
Twisting and turning dust devils
Like flamingo dancers
She whisked my heart away

For years I felt her warm embrace
Her cool breath upon my brow
Her heat against my bare skin
Our shared sweat in the sands

Our nights together
Days spent in shared exploration
Finding beauty everywhere
Discovering new depths to our love

Alas I was forced to leave you
To abandon our love forever
Forgive me Yuma
My desert temptress.

Dreams of You

I feel the heat from your body

The hot sweat not yet cooled

I slide my arm around you

Snuggling, our aroma lingers

Our bodies molded into one

Our exhaustion consumes us

I hear you softly crying

Your breathing is heavy

Chest heaving with desperate sobs

Touching my face you whisper

Do you love me

I answer that I do

Slowly we kiss

Tongues exploring once again

My hands searching every curve

Cautiously we let our emotions go

At the crescendo of our lovemaking

I awaken to find that once again

You have abandoned me.

Eternal Kiss

Dry your eyes try not to cry
Don't think that I will die
I just need to go away
In your heart I will always stay

I travel to a better place
Where heaven's light shines on my face
I will miss you my darling wife
But there's no pain in the afterlife

Should you ever get down or blue
Call my name and I'll come to you
My arms a comfortable glove
Enveloping you with my love

I pray you know that I love you
I'm sorry for what you went through
Please darling a final kiss for me
To hold me for eternity.

Eternal Love

I sit on packed wet sands
A beach with soothing waters
Located at the edge of the universe
The tides of salted tears flowing
Constantly carrying lost souls
Into the vast waters of eternity

I draw a picture of you
In the tear-stained sands
Hoping that I will find your soul
So we may travel forever
Across all eternity
In the tepid waters

As I pray for you
The tides wash the edges
My picture now my reflection
I realize that you too search
I release my soul into the water
To share eternity with you

As the sun sets
One last time on mankind
The waters of forgiveness
Carry us beyond the horizon
To an everlasting life
Of joy and love.

Eternally Yours

I crave those long nights
The blustery cold evenings
Snow piled high against the door
The fireplace our only warmth
My arms about you
Our bodies moving in unison
Sharing deep passionate kisses
Bodies glistening in the firelight
Our love reaching its summit
Then slowly sliding down
From heaven
Two hearts lying side by side
Feeling the heat from each other
Fire smolders to coals
We wrap ourselves together as one
I crave those long nights
But
You are no longer with me
You died
My love died
So I yearn now for the day
When we rekindle our love
Stoking the flames of our passion
Our souls reunited once more
Where our fire will burn for eternity

First Kiss

I met you one glorious day
At a dance you said I should stay
Talking and dancing throughout the night
Later we went out to get a bite

Taking a chance I held you tight
You didn't put up much of a fight
I got the chills at our first kiss
Closed my eyes no pleasures to miss

That is when I fell in love
And I prayed to God above
Please Lord bless us this day
Give a sign is what I prayed

Please Lord if she is to be mine
Then I ask that you give a sign
We opened our eyes only to see
That God had blessed both you and me.

Forbidden Places

I travel through the darkness
Looking for something
No... Someone
To guide me past the darkness
Through the wastelands
Into the depths of my soul

Suddenly you appear
You come in a dream
Together we travel the path
You bring enlightenment
An adept teacher
Ecstasy shared

Two hearts pounding
Sweat glistens
Exhausted bodies askew
You change our journey
Leading me onward
To forbidden places.

Freight Train Blues

Honey we tried real hard
But your cheating left me scarred
I go to work just to get away
I can't live these lies another day

> There's a freight train leaving town
> I'll be on it heaven bound
> Baby please don't cry for me
> I'm going home to Tennessee

I'm happy for you can't you see
You're exactly where you want to be
But here there is no room for me
I can't be the man you need me to be

> There's a freight train leaving town
> I'll be on it heaven bound
> Baby please don't cry for me
> I'm going home to Tennessee

I'll be up and gone before you wake
I've a train to catch and can't be late
A note on the table explaining why
Please my darling just say goodbye.

Goodbye To Love

Why did I stay with a broken heart
To you love was always À la cart
You took the good but not the bad
You drained me of everything I had

To you I was just a tool
No longer will I play your fool
Today I take back my heart
I deserve a brand-new start

I've pulled Cupid's arrow out of me
From this day on my heart is free
I think now it's your turn to cry
So to you I just say goodbye.

Harvest Moon

The harvest moon is shining
Up in the sky so bright
Two lovers entwined
Hearts soaring through the night

Shine on shine on
My beautiful harvest moon
Warming these two lovers
In each other's arms they swoon

The seed of love was planted
In fertile ground by moonlight
And when their passion passes
Guide them safely home this night

Some fifty years later
These lover's hearts still swoon
While sitting on a porch swing
Under their beautiful harvest moon.

I Am Here

I sit alone
Lost within my thoughts
Feelings flitter past
Memories just out of reach
My mind calls to them
Just when I think I've caught one
It darts away
Ever elusive
I remember
Nothing
What does it all mean
Why am I here
I feel abandoned
Forgotten by my own mind
You walk into the room
I know you, don't I
My brain is on fire
Shockwaves run through me
Memories bombard me
Who are you
I try to talk but I forget how
Suddenly
You look into my soul
My eyes shed but one tear
Your smile speaks volumes
I am here
You whisper into my ear
I will always be here.

I Remember You

I long for your kisses
You would roll onto me
Holding me down
Forcing my submission

I miss your hair
Falling across my face
As we laid in each other's arms
Your head nestled into my neck

I crave your soft touch
As you stroked my forehead
Ran fingers over my chest
Snuggling close to me

I remember your aroma
Honeysuckle shampoo
The taste of your lips
Your body entwined with mine

I cry every day for you
Praying for your return
Or for me to join you
In death.

In My Dreams

You came to me in a morning dream
With skin so white like fresh poured cream
The smoothness of alabaster skin
A hint of perfume as I breathe in
Sunlight glistening through corn silk hair
The sequenced dress I see you wear

I pray for you each night when I sleep
For you I'd give my heart to keep
Has someone finally answered my prayers
I can't look, fearing that you're not there

Opening my eyes and you've gone away
I'll have to suffer through another day
Shower water and tears look the same
I alone have to endure this pain
I feel emptiness deep inside
It's something that I must always hide

Today a new client I must meet
I swear she's the lady from my sleep
She looks at me eyes filling with tears
She's been searching for me many years

Fate can be fickle can't you see
I was shown to her and she to me
I came to her in her sleep
Fate chose the day we both would meet
Now when I dream, the only lady I see
Is my beautiful wife lying next to me.

In My Thoughts

I'm thinking of you
Are you thinking of me
We both have lived
Our pain and misery

No time to say goodbye
No time to just sit and cry
We both must carry on
Tomorrow's a brand-new dawn

I'll pray for you
You pray for me
I'll forever live in my misery
While you sleep for eternity.

Letter Home

I don't know what else I can do
So I've sent this letter home to you
It's the hardest thing for me to say
But my darling I must go away

I know it's hard but please don't cry
Daddy didn't want to die
I wish that we could still go and play
But my darling I must go away

You and Mommy will be just fine
And you can talk with me anytime
I will look down on you every day
But my darling I must go away

Soon you'll be grown and off to school
You'll always be Daddy's little jewel
Some boy will come steal your heart one day
But my darling I must go away

Someday you'll have a child too
A little girl who looks like you
When grandpa's name comes up one day
You say it's in your heart I stayed.

Lost Love

I sit down to write to her
She needs to know
Just how deeply I love her
Slowly tears drip onto paper
Blurring the pale blue ink
My soul mixes into the color
My tears become my words
Every memory every smile
The good times and the bad
All flow onto a single sheet
It is the story of our love
Two hearts beating as one
Years spent growing together
Supporting each other
Love that never dies
My words are done
I have written my heart
Sobbing, grief overcomes me
Sadly, I no longer remember
Who you are.

Lost Season

You whisper to me
Through the trees
Your breath moist
The scent of pine caresses
Relaxing my every sense

My eyes straining
Peering into the soft shadows
Trying to focus on your beauty
I could easily loose myself
Within you

I surrender to your charms
Your gentle embrace
You capture my heart
I cry out for you
I get shivers thinking of it

The night has chilled
I want to warm myself
To lie within your arms
But you have turned
You are a fickle lover

I feel your cold shoulder
Your wintry bite
I know I have lost you
Darkness consumes me
To a season without light.

Love

I see you in the doorway
Your hair sparkles in the light
Your beauty burns my eyes
Etched forever in my mind
Turning towards me
Your eyes look into my soul
Suddenly I am lost within you
I need your love

You show a perfect smile
I try rising to meet you, but
I'm captured by your gaze
Time slows, motions slow
But my heart is pounding
You glide seductively to me
Your radiance precedes you
Men are staring in vulgar awe

My pleasure senses explode
I can smell your sweet aroma
My passion erupts
I'm no longer in control
My temperature rises
My blood boils for you
With grace and poise
That perfect body bends

Our lips brushing lightly
You slide into the chair
My emotions fight for release
Reaching you take my hand
I can feel the flush
My words are slow to come
My darling you are beautiful
I'm so lucky you're my wife.

Love's Perils

I walk the narrow path
Along the edges
Between life and love

I peer over the precipice
Viewing loneliness and death
I struggle to keep my balance

But you are far above me
I inch closer to you
I reach for the pedestal

The rocks are sharp
Chinks appear in my defenses
Revealing my vulnerabilities

I offer you my crest
But you spurn me
Your words pierce my heart

My life blood drains
I collapse onto the crag
My body, my soul falling

Upon the jagged rocks of despair
Broken I lie alone
Never knowing love.

Love's Quest

As I cross the desert
Into the unknown
My thoughts are of you
I cannot help feeling
That we are forever lost
But I will cross this desert
Over the mountains
Through the deepest jungle
To find your heart again
I will change the river's course
Force the tides to recede
I will hold back time
And when our paths converge
In that unknown kingdom
Our hearts will unite
We can once again
Embrace our love
And travel through eternity
Together as one.

Making Memories

I watch carefully
As I walk across the sand
My footprints
Leaving behind impressions

The tides filling my divots
And the memory I left
Slowly fades with the backwash
My happiness washed away

What happens to my existence
Will it too be washed away
With the incoming tides
Like footprints in the sands

If I sit will my lifeblood
Wash slowly away with the tide
Has my destiny been preordained
Will I forever walk alone

Then I see you
Another soul on a quest
Was our meeting already written
We walk side by side

The tides are receding
Fresh sand appears
Two sets of footprints
Sharing memories in the sand.

Moving On

Have you ever really noticed
The state that I've been in
Used up my excuses
My alibis are mighty thin
I guess now that we're talking
It's time for me to come clean
I never wanted to hurt you
I'm really not that mean

For a long time now
I've been feeling that I'm all alone
Even when you're here with me
This really was not my home
Sometimes I catch you staring
Thinking my mind is gone
But really what I'm thinking
Is it's time for me to move on

I'll give you this house
It's the right thing to do
But ask no more of me
I'll give no more to you
After all the heartache and pain
That you have given me
Time for me to cut the bonds
If I'm to keep my sanity.

My Desert

I sit in solitude
In quiet contemplation
Feeling the warmth
From the morning sun
Eyes closed my skin tingles
From a sudden desert breeze

Listening I hear the thrasher
Singing its happiness for life
The desert has come alive
The lilies perfume
Filling my lungs
With her aroma of love

I look upon the desert
Her vastness dwarfs me
The cacti are in bloom
Drinking from the morning dew
The desert vultures flying high
Crows of the burning sands

I know my time is nigh
I close my eyes one last time
My soul escapes from my body
Soaring far above my love
She claims my body
To sleep with her for all of time.

My Regrets

Hello Mother it's Tommy look at me
I'm here to visit you can't you see
It's been a while since I last came
How are you doing, still the same

I've been so busy with the kids and wife
Not realizing the challenges of married life
That's no excuse for not seeing you
But with my new job I've much to do

With all my travels I have no time
Are the nurses good, you look just fine
We just got back from our big holiday
The theme park was great and the kids amazed

I don't understand the call from the home
They say you just sit here all alone
I should come more, maybe on Saturday
But the drive's quite long you're so far away

Mother your face is just a blank stare
You're scaring me now, are you in there
Has your condition worsened do you know me
Oh please, Mother please, say you forgive me

Hello Mother it's Tommy look at me
I'm here to visit you can't you see?

Passions

Your eyes sparkle
Reflections of a warm sun
On calm ocean waters

Your lips as deep a red
As ripened strawberries
Plump full of sweetness

Long auburn hair that reflects
The heat from the sun
Framing perfection

You reach out
Skin softer than alabaster
Drawing me to your bosom

Our lips lightly brush
A hint of your essence
The taste of your soul

I feel your smoldering breath
As you whisper in my ear
That you love me

You have captured me
My heart forever yours
Soon too my passion.

Secret In My Heart

You've been gone so many years
I stopped crying and dried my tears
Then she came after you were gone
She helped me to heal and move on
Little by little she pulled me away
Until suddenly I moved in one day

I feel emotions once again
Can she heal this heart full of pain
I'm scared not knowing what to do
I feel like I'm cheating on you

This lady has given her love to me
Second chances for our hearts to be free
You loved me in your special way
Yet I'm still lonely every day
You'd tell me to live, to make a new start
So I'll keep this secret deep in my heart.

Shared Memories

The smell of fresh cut grass
After a morning rain
Eating too much candy floss
A sugar rush to the brain
Riding on the Ferris wheel
A sweetheart on my arm
Remembering that first kiss
From a girl full of charm

We shared a lifetime
Those long summer days
When you had to move
I wished that you could stay
My broken heart would mend
Given a little time
I suppose it was written
That you would not be mine

To you I wish much happiness
A new beau and yes a ring
Maybe someday we'll meet again
To our families we shall cling
We'll just politely smile
A flash of memories it will bring
Of sitting atop that Ferris wheel
The kiss that made my heart sing.

Should I Go

There are times when I do not know
Should I stay or should I go
You said that you only loved me
You can't have me and still live free
I'm not trying to control you
But look at what you put me through

You go out forgetting your rings
Am I to know what your evening brings
Sometimes you're back so late at night
That's when my spirit says take flight

Should I stay or should I go
Times like this I do not know
I've been dead for an eternity
I guess it's time to just set you free
At least I now truly know
You'll be okay should I go.

Spring

Frost is on the window
There's fire in the hearth
Women in the back room
One is giving birth

A late-night winter storm
Is matching labor pains
Blowing snows are intensified
Like her strained and bulging veins

As the new day breaks
The storm has blown away
A beautiful newborn baby girl
Breathes life on an ordinary day

The warming rays of the sun
Shining through the window pane
While father and mother
Pick out cutesy baby names

Daddy says his little girl
Has brought the morning sun
Mother says she has a name
Thinking it should be the one

So Mother Nature tells him
To see if he likes the ring
She is my warmth and sunshine
I want to call her Spring.

Springtime

I see the song birds taking wing
Heralding in the coming spring
I see the bees flying hour on hour
Gathering nectar and seeding flowers

Lingering snow will soon fade away
With the warmth of the sun shining all day
Feeling the heat through the sunroom glass
I sit here all day reliving the past

People out walking the kids at play
They see me but have nothing to say
It's the season of romance and love too
But you need someone to share it with you

It was the coldest day of the year
When doctors relayed my worst fear
She's left me now to my own device
I felt my heart turn as cold as ice

That morning the skies cried tears of snow
The frozen drops on my cheeks didn't show
It took an eternity for me to drive home
Even less time to realize that I'm alone

The days run together the next like the last
Sitting in the sunroom behind weathered glass
Spring will never arrive for me
I buried my heart under an oak tree.

Stolen Heart

One day I awoke and you'd gone away,
The best part of me, died that day.
I remember now those days gone by,
How, both our branches touched the sky.
Strong branches and supple leaves,
Our life's blood sap upon which we'd feed.
Intertwined like soft silk lace,
Our leaves would touch each other's face.
The day you left you stole my soul.
Now here I stand, with a gaping hole,
The day you left I was torn apart,
Because when you left, it tore out my heart.

ESCAPING THE DARKNESS: RUNNING FROM MY DREAMS

Teddy Bear

I'm sitting here pondering
This crazy world in which I live
All the lonely people
Who have so much to give

As I reach into the pool
My old memories of life
To a time so long ago
Before I met my darling wife

As I reach down deeper
Into this oozing goo
I stop at a time
Long before I knew you

A scared young boy
That took beatings every day
Who grew into a man
Who chased people away

I pull my arms out slowly
From that memory goo
And stop upon the first time
That I laid eyes on you

You stabbed me in the heart
With that smile from ear to ear
Your honesty and openness
Melted all my fears

You never feared that man
With a temper black as sin
You found the chink in my armor
And snuck your love in

CHRISTOPHER BICE

I want to go lie now
Beside you on the bed
Wrap my arms around you
And kiss your sleeping head

You are my inspiration
Showing me all that I could be
And if we had never met
My heart would never be set free

You showed me that I could love
And the way we could share
So snuggle in closer
To this fierce old teddy bear.

The Crescent Moon

Two lovers entwined
Bathed by light from a crescent moon
Cool night breezes blowing
As their bodies swoon

Snuggled under a blanket
Drinking wine from a flask
Tickling each other's bodies
Sharing childish laughs

Fifty years of marriage
Never giving it a second thought
Same as it was many years ago
Chancing they might get caught

Their love coming full circle
Beneath the crescent moon
Where two old lovers
Under a blanket still swoon.

The Dream

I lived a dream
You were gone
Searching I call your name
My heart pounding with fear
Our love flashed before me
Life dims, fades to black
Unable to control my emotions
I awake my pillow wet with tears
Softly sobbing, body convulsing
My grief consuming me
Begging for forgiveness
Praying for a second chance
My mind and body in fetal
Why am I being punished
Where have you gone
Suddenly feeling your closeness
You slide your arm around me
Feeling your hot breath on my neck
You whisper what's wrong
Nothing I say, nothing at all
I just lived a dream.

The Gift

I sit by the campfire
Its embers are softly glowing
The heat still caresses me
I am content in the cold air

Looking up I see the stars
My breath becomes a veil
I ask aloud if you are real
Show a sign so I may know

A star shoots across the sky
Still my mind resists
Why do I hesitate
A sign was given

Why me Lord
Why do you care
Why do I doubt you
How can I truly know

I see you in the moonlight
A silhouette in the doorway
I now know His love is real
Because He sent you to me.

The Jungle

I have arrived in this concrete jungle
I make my way to the watering hole
You arrive hesitating in the doorway
The sun glistening through your hair

A halo of light framing a perfect angel
I am immediately smitten
Your beauty is beyond compare
Our eyes meet volumes are spoken

Leaving your friends you come to me
My throat contracts in anticipation
You smile seeing my innocence
Pheromones of spiced honeysuckle

Capturing my heart you draw me in
You brush against me sealing my fate
Heart spinning, like dust devils back home
Ordering your drink, I hear the music

You are playing a love song to me
Smiling I pay, its tribute to your beauty
You leave. My heart now a prize in hand
Only the strong survive in the jungle.

The Lazy River

As one's life meanders
Down the lazy river
Of time

How one rides
Occasional rapids
Is how one is defined

The inner tube
Of your happiness
May find a hidden stick

At times like those
You must have a plan
To implement real quick

One prays for help
That one's ride
Will always float along with ease

That life's tensions
Will be forgotten
With a warm summer breeze

And when one sees
The lazy river's mouth
Leading to the sea

The journey
Was made much more fun
When you tubed along with me.

The Looking Glass

I look into the mirror and I don't see me
I see instead your radiance shimmering back
My heart melts and releases my essence
You have captured my soul and grounded me
My limbs stretching reaching for your love
I need to feel your perfect embrace
I crave that subtle caress upon my face
I can almost feel your tickles in the breeze
You are callously flirting and teasing me
My emotions and passions are fueling my desires
I imagine us intertwined in perfect harmony
In my mind I relive our ecstasy
My soul screams out needing only you
But alas I hear your whispers in the wind
That our love was not meant to be
Peering deeper into the depths of the mirror
I am but a pebble causing ripples in your heart

The Lovers

A lover's moon is out tonight
Secret rendezvous out of sight
Innocent banter a brush of an arm
Stealing away wouldn't cause any harm

Playful tongues the adventure begins
Consensual love breaks the seventh sin
Two hearts beating playing out a tune
Crescendo of passion lovers' swoon

Bodies entwined like a serpent's dance
Pleasured cries while they're entranced
Hot breath across glistening skin
The passion builds deep within

The guttural moans the stifled cries
Passions released from deep inside
Lovers meeting beneath a cheating moon
Pledging another secret meeting soon.

The Painting

I look at you looking at me
You move slowly to and fro
Glancing away occasionally
But your eyes always return

To me for what seems like hours
I too watch you
My eyes following your every move
I sit motionless as I ponder

How life for you must be
How busy you are
You seem so consumed
So vibrant with purpose

While I waste my life away
Fading in the sunlight
You made of flesh and blood
Me trapped on the canvas

Forever staring
At the passerby's going past
Wishing I could live
Other than just on this wall

ESCAPING THE DARKNESS: RUNNING FROM MY DREAMS

The Sonnet

I sit upon the sand
By an ocean of salted tears
Writing in powdered glass
A great sonnet of joy and love

Remembering our life, our love
Tears of joy flowing
Creating rivulets through my words
Blurring memories

Torrents of thought washing over me
I'm drowning in my mind
Whispers bombarding me
Fighting for breath

Waves of despair
Eroding my mind
Staring at the sands of time
My words are fading

The tide changes
Cleansing my mind of you
My sonnet now unwritten
Just teardrops on a clean slate.

The Voyage

A gifted person once said that, "Love is never having to say you're sorry." This statement is completely wrong. Love is wanting, needing, to say you're sorry. To be able to communicate with your lover, that you'll always regret any misgivings or mistakes you've made which may offend, hurt or do harm in any way to the relationship which is the biggest treasure you have.

Imagine a long journey down a winding river. This is the river of life, sometimes smooth calm waters flowing, winding, and gently caressing the shores as it makes its way eventually to the sea, to join with a bigger, more adventurous body of water, the ocean. Sometimes this river meets turbulence with hidden dangers lurking just beyond your sight, rocks or hidden limbs waiting to catch your love and slowly drag it down to obscurity, to drown in sorrow, despair and loneliness.

Often one wishes for a paddle or a life preserver to save themselves from the perils of love but none is needed. The true challenge is to allow the currents of emotion, the passions of the minute to carry you further along your voyage. Riding the eddies and navigating the white water of true love allows you to move more quickly to your final port, to journeys end.

Braving the waters of love, allowing yourself to be swept through your life to the ocean is the only way to experience life to its fullest. For what is life without love? Without love my life is nothing. Sailing the river of life becomes much more spiritual, when there are two souls navigating the rapids and the deep pools together.

So, to you I say, I'm sorry, I'm sorry, I'm sorry. I never meant for you to be hurt or alone. I regret not having met sooner so our journey could have started together. I apologize for not being your life jacket. Luckily for me we met at the tributaries of love where souls join the river of life and we were able to lash our vessels to brave the waters together. My longing for a companion on my long voyage has finally appeared and together we can watch the horizon, looking forward to the mouth of passion, the final opening to the ocean's arms. I wish only smooth sailing today and for the rest of your life.

Time Moves On

Time is motion

Tic toc

Tic toc

The seconds passing

Minutes gaining speed

Another hour passes

Another day, week, year

If I could hold time

In a bottle

If I could control time

Turn back the sun dial

Daylight savings

But time moves forward

Marching to its own beat

Timed out

Times up

If I could've stopped time

I could have saved you.

Tinker Bell

Tinker tinker my tinker bell

You got up when you fell

Try again with all your might

Try once more to get it right

Practice hard so the better you'll be

Soon to fly with Mom and Me

Soon your heart will soar and fly

Your wings will take you to the sky

Tinker tinker my tinker bell

I'm so proud you tried when you fell.

Twilight Prayers

Sitting at the shoreline
I watch the sun slowly die
The horizon consumes it
Memories fading to black

Each day a new sunrise
For me a new birth
Brand new memories
That sometimes slip away

Today I met you
I fell in love
Desperately I want to live
Forever in this moment

But the sun is setting
My memories dip beneath
An all-consuming horizon
I pray for dawn once again.

Vampire Love

You've sucked all the love out of me
You're just a vampire can't you see
Oh you can come into the light
But from you it just takes one bite

Seductive clothes with a body that kills
Seeing you gives every man the chills
They all fight just to try and meet you
When you sink your fangs, what can they do

You'll suck all their life from them
Then find someone new and do it again
You've grown rich off the men you bleed
Houses, cars and whatever you need

Someday Cupid's arrow will find you
That shaft of wood will end you too
It will kill the vampire deep within
That's when your new life can begin

I pray I'm around on that day
When your demons are chased away
I'll be so happy to see your new start
Because you still own a piece of my heart.

Where Angels Walk

Angels walking up and down the rows

Looking for lambs amongst the lost souls

When they find one, they take them by the hand

Leading them glory bound to the Promised Land

I shall never fear should I fall in this troubled land

I'll just wait my turn to take my angel's hand

Winter's Rest

Tis not death, just a long winter's sleep
So hold your tears, for me don't weep
I'll awaken transformed and splendid come spring
The beauty you see will come on wing.

Wishes

I feel your fingers wisp
lightly across my cheek
With a breeze you shush me
as I begin to speak
Your perfume quietly
invading my soul
Slowly toward you
I begin to roll

Carefully opening my eyes
only to find
The reality that you live
just in my mind
This the anniversary
of the day
When my heart was
suddenly called away

So here I lie
crying today
Praying tonight
that you might stay
My dearest wife
I miss you so
Take my heart with you
when you go.

Your Evil Ways

I saw you on the corner
looking like a ten
All the boys are staring
you're winking at the men

But I know you all too well
the way you use those body parts
You draw all the men to you
and break those poor boy's hearts

Chorus
> I'll fight to win you over
> to change your evil ways
> Soon it will be my turn
> to break your heart and walk away

Soon the day will come
when you're on the outside looking in
Thinking of all the hearts you broke
the years living full of sin

When you're feeling lonely
like you've lost someone along the way
Look for me on that corner
it's now my turn to make you pay

Chorus
> I'll fight to win you over
> to change your evil ways
> Soon it will be my turn
> to break your heart and walk away.

DEATH

A Child's Remorse

Come home drunk again today
More black eyes given away
Or maybe this time a broken bone
Mother and child praying all alone

A trip to have a doctor see
'Dunno Doc the kid's clumsy'
A child crying dry tears
Living life full of fears

School with bruises purple and black
Teachers report a vicious attack
Child services come take him away
But his Mother is forced to stay

Drunker than he's ever been
Neighbors hear a painful scream
A shot rings out in the night
A Mother has lost her fight

A child screams out in pain
It's all my fault once again
Why didn't you leave me alone
I deserve to be with Mom at home.

A Promise

Children running up the block
On Sunday morning sidewalks
Girls wearing a pretty Easter dress
Boys sporting bow ties and fancy vests

Going to church and Sunday schools
Parents teaching the golden rules
Families gather to say their prayers
Wanting forgiveness their souls to spare

Vows between a husband and wife
Allowing God into their life
Love bound with a golden ring
Holding hands on a settee swing

Watching as the children go by
The old man begins to cry
Their children grown and moved away
Promising to come back some day

Years of sadness he wished were gone
Now alone since his wife passed on
God promised he'd see her again
That his heart would feel no more pain

Slowly the old man closes his eyes
To worldly troubles he says goodbye
She waits for him on a settee swing
He always cherished his golden ring.

Always

Please sit I've something to say
Not too long till I go away
I wish I could leave you money or gold
But my treasures are of us growing old

It'll get easier as time goes by
Hush my darling please don't cry
My heart will be with you every day
At night I'll lie with you as you pray

Plant a rose in the garden by the tree
In the spring when it blossoms think of me
In the heat of the summer I'll be there
It's my warm embrace you feel in the air

Autumn colors are painting the trees
Remember our laughter raking the leaves
In the winter stay cozy here in our home
I'm the warmth of the fire you're never alone

Please live and laugh my darling run free
When you're ready come home to me
We'll share everlasting life just wait and see
A seat at his table awaits you, with me.

Black Lake

I dip my quill
Into the living vessel
Of my arm

As the blood drips
The pen scratches
Weathered parchment

I write my love
But the ink
Turns black

My sonnets
My songs
Run together

My world blurs
So too my words
My life force spills

The vessel empties
Blood drowns
My words of love

Into a pool
At the bottom
Of the parchment

Forgotten words
Lying at the bottom
Of a black lake.

Broken Lines

I float between the realms
Crossing the broken lines
Feeling love freely given
But never reciprocated

Memories soon forgotten
When I passed over
Then time stood still
For one fleeting moment

Inspiration appeared
A heavenly encounter
A glimpse into perfection
Before a harsh reminder

Of a chaos brought forth
To an innocent world
A soul charred black
Cast into madness.

Catching A Cloud

I cast my line to a cloud
Hoping to catch a ride
Through expansive skies
To find you again

I scan the heavens
I search the earth
Desperately looking
Wondering where you are

Finally, my cloud finds you
Slowly it darkens
Angry at your death
I am no longer in control

My heart breaks
My soul cries tears
Soaking your grave
With my life's blood

As the bleeding slows
I cast for another cloud
Praying it will fly me
Forever into your arms.

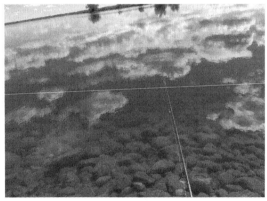

Chiseled In Stone

A warm summer evening
a breeze is in the air
Opening a window
her scent is everywhere
I boil up the kettle
to make myself a tea
I made it home safely
so certain she'd be pleased
Joining other couples
friends that we both knew
Awkward conversations
they've not lived what I've been through
They think it's easy
for me to come here alone
But it's not their wife's name
that just got chiseled in stone.

Daddy

A clear plastic tent over you
Daddy what must you be going through
Mom cries by your bedside every day
Daddy I wish we could still go play

Chorus
      Daddy when are you coming home
      Mommy can't take being alone
      And me I just cry for you every day
      Daddy why couldn't you just stay

I know you had to be alone
That God came down to take you home
You were sick and stayed away
But I missed you every day

      Daddy when are you coming home
      Mommy can't take being alone
      And me I just cry for you every day
      Daddy why couldn't you just stay

But now you're gone, you'll not be home
You left Mom and me all alone
But don't forget that we love you
I'll take care of Mom we'll get through

      Daddy when are you coming home
      Mommy can't take being alone
      And me I just cry for you every day
      Daddy why couldn't you just stay.

Death Of A Child

I awake my eyes wet
My pillow damp with sorrow
Uncontrollable sobbing
Realizing that again I dreamt of him

That small child
An innocent boy
Forced to remain locked up
A captive of his own mind

His anguish and pain visible
He's fighting but not for life
He pleads for an end
No longer can he survive

His conflicts are insurmountable
Death is his only release
I sit by his side as he passes
Crying openly for this lost soul

Stumbling to the bathroom
I stare at the reflection in the mirror
No longer do I see a youthful face
Instead a man looks back at me

The inner child euthanized
His life forfeited
Manhood thrust upon him
My innocence stolen by life.

Dream

I dreamed a dream where I died

People came but no one cried

Saying I was a good man

But my poems were all unplanned

They burned my works page by page

Branding me as too new aged

Here I lie in this cold dark earth

No more works will I ever birth

So shed a tear for me because I died

Never a poet but at least I tried.

Electric Dreams

I stare at an electric fire
Dreaming electric dreams
Watching cold flames
Dancing before my eyes
Hinting at warmth
Broken promises

Putting in time
Years wasted
Fighting for a dream
Life's merry-go-round
Reaching for a gold ring
Broken promises

My mind plays tricks
Memories flooding
So many tears
Drowning my flame
Whispers in my ear
Broken promises

The golden years
A time for comfort
Pensions stolen
One room shack
Warmth from an electric fire
Broken promises.

Going Home

I lie in this hospital bed
Knowing that soon I'll be dead
Some may cry and some might grieve
But who will miss me when I leave

None of my children are here today
It seems that I've outlived my stay
An apparition I suddenly see
My wife has finally come for me

My life flashing before my eyes
I see my wife beginning to cry
We've had many smiles and some tears
You've waited for me all these years

"I've come for you Honey can't you see
You always were the best part of me"
I'm afraid to go. I'm afraid to die.
"Let go of this life, just say goodbye"

The pain forces me to moan
"My love I'm here to take you home
Rest husband, she says as she weeps
Just close your eyes and go to sleep"

Yes my love I'll go home with you
I've just one last thing I must do
Now I lay me down to sleep
I pray thee Lord my soul to k_ _ _.

Home Again

I remember as a child sent out to play
For me the summers were glorious days
Playing cowboys and army tag
Winners, losers, both still bragged
Blood brothers' friends for life
Both fearing the cut of the knife

Grade school allowed us time to play
Until my best friend moved away
I watched as the moving truck left that day
Vowing never again to be hurt that way

At high school I was always alone
Hormones raging, I reaped what was sown
A fight that I took a bit too far
My new home, a room behind bars
Two years lost being a fool
But I learned much, in that school

A freak accident took my parents away
I no longer had any reason to stay
I left that day the highways to roam
Knowing it was the last time I'd see home

Stopped somewhere along the way
Got a job and a place to stay
Thought I was in love and took a wife
Found she was living a secret life
So once again I took to the road
Working odd jobs to buy white gold

Excitement pulsing through my vein
It's a release from trouble and pain
I've done things of which I'm not proud

CHRISTOPHER BICE

Living life under a cold black shroud

A secret was nagging me every day
I longed for those summer days at play
The liquid gold allowed me to dream
The more I took the more real it seemed

Tonight, I decided I wanted to play
So in my dreams forever I would stay
Tears of joy running down my face
Home again to my special place
My spirit soared as I started to twitch
I left this cruel world face down in a ditch.

I'm Coming Home

I got the call to go down the road
Off to fight for some unwritten code
Finally there's no more misery or pain
My darling girl I'm coming home again

    So come down from the hills
    And into the glen
    Open your heart
    Let love in again
    My darling forever here I will stay
    No more will I ever run away

No longer weary I've come home by train
No band to greet me in the driving rain
I'm fast asleep lying in the back
Riding in my carriage painted black

    So come down from the hills
    And into the glen
    Open your heart
    Let love in again
    My darling forever here I will stay
    No more will I ever run away

So lie me down in our precious glen
Come visit with me now and then
Please continue to live and love every day
Darling dry your tears as you walk away

    So come down from the hills
    And into the glen
    Open your heart
    Let love in again
    My darling forever here I will stay

CHRISTOPHER BICE

No more will I ever run away

My darling forever here I will stay
No more will I ever run away.

Little White Lie

Teardrops on my pillow
Moonbeams blind my eyes
We never got the chance
To say all of our goodbyes

Robbed of our tomorrows
You were taken by surprise
I'll never really understand
You told me those white lies

How can I go on living
Moving forward every day
How do I tell our children
That mommy's gone away

Teardrops on my pillow
Moonbeams blind my eyes
Darling I wish you were here
And I was the one that died.

Masks

Today which mask will I wear
Do I show my emotions bare
Should I chance that others will see
The pain and suffering inside me

Wearing many masks to hide my pain
I couldn't bear being hurt again
My heart has now turned to stone
Since you left me here alone

Tomorrow may be a brand-new day
No masks left to hide my pain away
You know the sorrow I've been through
My love I can't live without you

Tonight I leave this lonely place
My death mask is my smiling face
No tears on my pillow will you see
We'll be together for eternity.

Missing You

No one to turn to when I need to cry
So I'll bury my feelings deep inside
Full of self-pity and anger too
Who should I blame for losing you

Thinking our love would always be there
I skipped through life without a care
I should have said I love you every day
But now it's too late you've gone away

I was too stupid to see the signs
Always thinking we'd have better times
You hid your sadness inside of you
I didn't know what you were going through

No longer is this house a home
When one is forced to live alone
Here in my castle, I'll hide in shame
Knowing deep inside that I'm to blame

You hid your fears so skillfully
You always tried to protect me
I promised you we'd never be apart
Tomorrow with you, I bury my heart.

Monsters

Golden ringlets hanging
Alongside your perfect face
Eyes still moist now closing
Tears of sorrow drying
You are a mirror
Reflecting your Mother's beauty
Sleep my precious child
Daddy is here
To fight off the monsters
That haunt your dreams
But who battles my monsters
When I shut my eyes
How can I fill the void
That giant sinkhole
That crushed my heart
I awake feeling your arms
Wrapped around my neck
Together we share our tears
You are here for me
We fight each other's monsters
Battling our grief together
Our shared losses
A Wife, a Mother
Gone.

My Best Friend

As I lie here
In this hospital bed
Someone brings my dog
To lie beside my head
That little pup of mine
Is overwhelmed with joy
I turn my head to say
He's such a good boy

Carefully he snuggles in
Then gives a heavy sigh
I think that he knows
That this is our last goodbye
With my last strength
I lay my hand upon his side
I'm so glad you're here
Both of us are teary eyed

My friend stayed with me
The rest of that day
Never left my side
When the priest came to pray
Suddenly he started howling
As I slowly slipped away
Holding off my demons
Until an angel takes me home to stay.

The Closet

My closet is a safe place to hide
I don't allow anybody inside
Conversations in the night
I know I don't feel quite right
The darkness hides my fears
No witnesses to my tears

My feelings hidden I try to pray
But it seems he has turned away
Acting normal throughout the day
My inner demons held at bay

So called friends make fun of me
I shared my secrets can't they see
Obscene whispers as I pass by
Force me to hide so I can cry
Walking through the halls in school
Everyone knows. I'm such a fool

So I walk these streets alone
Too afraid of going home
Parents who think it's just a phase
They don't hear me, won't meet my gaze

My closet is a safe place to hide
I don't allow anybody inside
Conversations in the night
I know I don't feel quite right
Grief and pain have won this fight
Who will miss this loser's life?

My Goodbye

I sit in an empty room
My mind full of regrets
My heart empty
Devoid of love
My soul crushed

Awaking each day alone
With new levels of sorrow
My guilt a shackle
Forever binding me
Anchoring me

My pain consumes me
It's my fault I am the cause
How can I live this way
I created this nightmare
It can never be undone

Can I be undone
There's no way out
Perhaps it's easier
Just to let go
To say…..goodbye.

New Day

Another new day
I awake on a floor
Still too stoned to walk
I crawl through the door
Stumbling to find a bus stop
The sun burning my eyes
My head about to explode
My thoughts of food
Quickly replaced by my needs

Cravings that consume me
There across the street
A convenience store
An easy mark for fast cash
Still stumbling I pull the knife
From my right boot
My demands are made
The man behind the counter
Looks familiar

I've been here before
He's mumbling something
I see a gun
But my hunger consumes me
A queer sensation
Deep within my chest
My hunger leaves me
I smile a smile of thanks
My pain has been taken away.

Nuclear Wind

The fields are all dead
Crops no longer grow
Brackish water lies
Black death where ripples flow

Toxic winds are blowing
Across a morning sky
Acid rain is falling
On ground that's always dry

Mother Nature was murdered
A long time ago
A thousand years later
And still this ashen snow

What became of mankind
When the world became a grave
Only the worst survived
Deep down in concrete caves.

Saying Goodbye

I feel the dark clouds
They hang above my head
Lightning strikes my eyes
I feel that I am dead

Stumbling through the darkness
An ill wind pushing me
I find you laying there
I wish we both could flee

But you were the chosen
And all of us must stay
The memory of your love
Will help us through each day

The torrent now comes
But not from the skies
It's caused from the pain
Of saying our goodbyes

The sun will come again
And chase the clouds away
You'll never be forgotten
In our hearts you will always stay.

Song Birds

I listen hard for the song birds to sing
Heralding in the coming of spring
The sun will be much higher in the sky
I long to see pretty birds flying by

Tweeting young hatchlings crying for food
Mother keeps busy feeding this brood
These young ones too will take wing
Flying, one will hear them sing

With the clouds parting in the sky
These song birds are soaring quite high
They sing of hope and forgiveness you see
But none of these things were given to me

Here I lie in a cold dark grave
A man who took more than he gave
Evil black ravens now sing to me
Cawing on my bones incessantly.

The 5 W's

Who is the darkness
Who is the light
Who started it
Who wins the fight

What was the reason
What was the cause
What really happened
What caused us to pause

Where will we go
Where will we hide
Where have the people gone
Where is their guide

When will this be over
When can we leave home
When can we chance
When can we roam

Why did this happen
Why did the earth cry.
Why didn't we listen
Why did we die.

The Final Round

A war of words again tonight
Tears through stained black eyes
A son fighting for his life
Parents parry in the ring
Pale greyness, a suffering child
Eyes glazed like translucent milk
Open potholes visible
Down the roadways in his arm
Machines keeping death away
Chill reminders of a morgue
The sudden ringing of a bell
Round two has now begun
Alone in the crowded room
The patient slips away
While parents continue fighting
Both not claiming any blame
The final round now over
The alarms now turned off
A child who lost his fight
Not knowing love at all.

The Last Kiss

He ran his fingers through her grey streaked hair
It was a badge of honor she was proud to wear
She always maintained that she was in style
Thinking of the good times he slowly smiled

She raised our kids and yes, she even tamed me
We made a life together, started our family tree
The hard times behind us, the kids moved away
Starting their trees; we have grandchildren today

At family gatherings they come home you see
Like Thanksgiving and Christmas, we all help with the tree
They're all coming home for the gathering today
I'll be happy to see them, hoping they won't rush away

Family and friends have all come around
Father Murphy is standing, he's sermon bound
Usually it's fire, brimstone and Hell
Today it's a softer story he'll tell

Where angels come hither and sing
A kindred spirit home they will bring
At the end of the eulogy there's not a dry eye
Even I shudder as I begin to cry

Go to rest my pretty darling, you had to leave
But we'll be together soon for eternity
I'm kneeling one last time at your side
Where I'll give you, our last kiss, goodbye.

The Last Score

I walk these dark streets alone
Hours before I need to go home
I have to have one more score
My body craves more and more

My burning stomach won't go away
Just one more score to end my day
I stagger into the bad side of town
This is where my last fix will be found

People always see me as a threat
My body shivers in a cold sweat
Just one more fix to end my day
Then I promise to just hide away

Down the street an alley I see
Maybe there's a fix there for me
Yes there's a pusher down there
He gives me an evil stare

I tell myself it's my last score
The rest of the day I'll need no more
My stomach screaming its hunger pangs
As into his neck I sink my fangs.

The Long Road Home

It's time for me to head back home
I've traveled these roads all alone
I left friends and family behind
I roamed the world my fortune to find

For many years my homes were just cheap rooms
Sleeping mat, a meal, for an hour pushing broom
Looking for a roof overhead when all else failed
A drunken fight in a bar to sleep in a jail

Caught malaria and scarlet fever as well
Live or die doctors said; "only time will tell"
I've seen my share of women and I've loved a few
What kind of life could I give them my time's coming due

So one last time I travel these roads going home
To see family and friends never more will I roam
Somewhere in my travels a deadly illness found me
Coming home looking for forgiveness to set me free

My family and friends will never know
At best I've maybe got six months to go
I'll fill them with many years of stories over a beer
I'll live my six months like I've got twenty more years

When my time approaches and everyone's here
I'll give a rousing toast and hoist my last beer
They all think that I no longer wanted to roam
They may be right I want to be buried at home.

The Promise

Sixty years ago, I gave you my heart
We said our vows, never to be apart
Sharing ourselves through good and bad
Living through your death left me so sad
I buried you with my heart that day
You've gone ahead to pave the way

Every night I lie in our bed and weep
Until finally I cry myself to sleep
My head on your pillow I smell your perfume
I catch glimpses of you smiling in the room

I've laid your favorite dress out on the bed
Kneeling to pray, in your lap is my head
I promised to stay with you all of our days
And this loneliness I feel just won't go away
I can't live with this anguish inside my head
I pray that God takes my soul to you instead.

The Taste Of Sorrow

Who is it I whispered
The fire glowed a freakish green blue
Who is it I plead hoarsely
A shadow glides closer
A wraithlike creature appears
My stomach recoils in terror
The bile rising to my mouth
The specter leans forward
A face slowly appears
By the light of the last embers
I could see her clearly
My lost love
Gone these many years
Slowly she sinks down
Back to the blackness
Into the ashes of the fire
To the abyss of despair
Steam sizzles
My soul dripping from wet eyes
The embers now dead
Her loss is once more felt
My body convulses in agony
I lie down my face buried deep
I'm breathing the dank coals
Sorrow tastes like the ashes of death.

The Tempest

The pounding rain the driving hail
A raging tempest that rips the sails
The brutal winds and thirty-foot seas
A sailor prays to Poseidon to appease

Another raging tempest not of the sea
Her violent anger cannot be appeased
The chill down his spine his prickling hair
Praying to the God's his life to spare

As if in answer the violence subsides
The sailor submits with tear filled eyes
Fears like this he would never see
When he sailed his boat upon the seas

Now a sea of grain and a small log home
Day and night working fingers to the bone
With sickle and scythe he stacks the grain
Dreaming secretly to unfurl his sails again

With the grain all in, it's a blustery night
For his tempest at home, he has given his life
For her he'd come home and furled his sails
But the tempest of the deep for him still wails

Death took the old sailor late one night
His tempest at home has lost her fight
She commits him to the lady of the deep
The tempest of the sea his soul will keep.

Time

Like sands in an hourglass

Falls slowly to rest below

Life too rests

Reset the sand

Start over

Birth

Life begins

The children grow

Everyone gets old

Time keeps moving onward

Sand flows time always wins

ESCAPING THE DARKNESS: RUNNING FROM MY DREAMS

Wanted Dead Or Alive

The sun beats down on the desert plain
A cowboy breaks camp once again
The last of his water he gives to his horse
He's praying it will stay the course

One long day they still must ride
To the mountains on the westward side
Scorpions and rattlers along the way
All kinds of perils to spoil the day

There's a hidden pass up ahead
A dry gulch area where fools lie dead
Thieves and scoundrels lie in wait
For hapless folk to take the bait

This cowboy has come this way before
He'll not be lured into Hell's back door
He decides to take the long way around
It'll bring him in on the far end of town

By then the sun will be dipping down
It's definitely the best way into town
The sun will be shining at his back
He'll be able to see a surprise attack

He reaches the old livery barn
He's come this far without too much harm
Saddle off and horse has been fed
Time for a quick drink before bed

A saloon and dance hall across the street
Perfect place to wet his whistle with a drink
Enjoying his drink with a girl at his side
Through the mirror he sees the doors open wide

CHRISTOPHER BICE

In walks a mountain of a man
He spies the cowboy and forms a plan
He'll goad this cowboy into a fight
This trail bum is going to die tonight

This man came to force a duel
Thinking just to kill some poor fool
The cowboy's hand dropped at the speed of light
That big man is the one that died tonight

The people in the saloon clapped and cheered
The man dead on the floor was one they feared
The cowboy pulled a badge from out of his vest
And he pinned it on so all could attest

He said he'd hoped to save them from bloodshed
But big Joe Bostwick was wanted alive or dead
I'm Harry Wheeler an Arizona Ranger, see
I'm guessing Big Joe will now come along peacefully.

INSPIRATION

A Christmas Prayer

Here I sit so sad and lonely
No one waiting at home for me
So I sit on this bench and cry
Waiting patiently just to die

Season's come and seasons go
Through driving rain and cold
You can always find me here
For me, Christmas holds no cheer

I lost my job my home my wife
So much pain to endure in one life
Half my life spent feeling screwed
I crawl through dumpsters for food

Oh my a goldmine found in here
Half a burger fries and part beer
As I'm enjoying my feast tonight
I realize something's not quite right

The bell tower strikes half past three
That's when a glow surrounds me
I see a man walking my way
I'm so scared I start to pray

Be calm my friend he says to me
I've come this night to set you free
It's Christmas Eve and I cannot stay
What is the one thing for which you pray

The thing I've wanted in this life
Is to see again my darling wife
Are you sure that's all you desire
That's when I heard a heavenly choir

CHRISTOPHER BICE

Look down the alley, what do you see
Please tell me my eyes don't deceive me
Is that my wife walking this way
Lord grant my wish with her to stay

A Christmas miracle given just for me
From this miserable life God set me free
My husband, no more will you be alone
Come my love; take my hand we're going home.

An Honest Man

I awoke to a world where I was alone
Others too were there but it's wasn't home
I was born into grief and misery
Survived using my fists and trickery

The other children knew to watch out for me
When the blackness came their blood ran free
In my darkest hour you rescued me
When you took me home you set me free

I was never an easy child to raise
Always in trouble I needed no praise
In and out through juvenile hall
Why would you stay through it all

You stuck with me arms open wide
A weaker person would have died
I'm almost through my teenage years
I know I've heard you cry many tears

You loved me through the good and bad
I would have drove lesser person mad
I'm standing with adoption papers in hand
if you'll have me, you raised an honest man.

Ballerina

Pretty ballerina won't you dance for me
You're up on your tippy toes I can't believe
You float all across the stage
Watching you I'm totally amazed

You spin and twirl in the breeze
Your sole purpose is just to please
I come back almost every day
To watch you dance your time away

In the garden where you grow
You are the hit of the show
Your dance troupe dances too
Next year I'll plant more of you.

Little Blue Pony

Little blue pony of the sea
Carry my soul away for me
They committed my body to the deep
For the Goddess Amphitrite to keep

I pray that she'll release me
Spread my particles evenly
And now I make one last wish
Allow my husk to feed the fish

When I was alive, I sailed the seas
Praying Poseidon to watch over me
He provided my bounty all my life
Gave me a ship and a beautiful wife

My mortal life above I'll not miss
My Lady there gave me her last kiss
So here I rest snuggled deep in your cool wet sands
Blue pony carry my soul to the Promised Land.

Choices

Eyelids heavy from sleep
Still I force them to open
Before me stands a dark clad man
I try to speak but cannot
Slowly his arm moves
Pointing to a hallway

A silk veil covers the entrance
I rise and cross to the veil
With a rush of cool wind
The veil slips away

Peering within this realm
I see ecstasy
I feel the burning
Deep within my loins
My heart pounds
I cry with the passion

A second veil looms
Pulling it aside I peer into it
Therein lies power beyond compare
I feel untouchable...supreme

The last veil is opaque
I quiver with anticipation
This realm shows possibilities
But also comes with finality
I must choose a veil
It is solely my decision

The dark clad man confronts me
I see the knife that penetrates my chest
With piercing pain my eyes open
Knowing my choice has been made.

Daisies

I walk across the fields
And witness the daisies
Craning for a bit of sun
As they poke their faces
Through a fresh blanket of snow

Soon they will sleep
To be reborn in spring
Taking nourishment
From the melting snow
To again smile in the sunshine

And the thought comforts me
That I too may be reborn
To live again in heaven's field
Drinking from the wellspring
That is God's love.

Darkness

What is darkness
Do the wicked hide there
Does it corrupt the mind
Preying on weakness
Is it the birth place of evil
A way to steal your soul
Does death still rule the night

Or is it just an absence of light
But what then is light
Can it be pure joy
Is it strictly illumination
For the visionaries
Does it free your soul
Will the light save all mankind

Can light survive without darkness
Does the darkness not need light
Are they not two halves of a coin
The yin and yang of the universe
Were we not given the choice
Man controls his own destiny
To flip the switch on or off.

ESCAPING THE DARKNESS: RUNNING FROM MY DREAMS

Desert Breath

The coldest month of the year
And the desert whispers its cool breath
Across the plains

The days are getting longer
The afternoons warmer
The nights still jacket cool

A fine dust floats in the air
Looking for unsuspecting homes
Breathe deep smell the aromas

Cactus blooms lingering
Awaiting the warm desert spring
Hoping for the first drink

The fine dust coats everything
My mouth, my throat
Even my eyes feel its touch

Slowly I dip beneath
The warm waters
Refreshing myself

Resting along the pool side
Margarita in hand
I listen to its whispers.

Distant Drums

In the hills I hear the distant drums
Proclaiming the 'One' has finally come
The twelve drummers drumming
A celebration is coming

In the heavens and on earth
All will praise His holy birth
God has given his only Son
So all our sins will be undone

So on this holy Christmas morn
Our trees of life we all adorn
Shining bright that all may see
So thankful that we are sin free

A great feast will await me and you
A seat at His table for just a few
All from a miracle that set us free
The birth of a partridge in a pear tree

Doorway

On a stainless slab
I lay waiting
For the first incision
The one that will save me
My heart racing
My mind praying

A sudden calmness
As anesthetic soothes
Echoes in my mind
Calling to me
Memories of a life
Dreams of yesteryears

I see the veils
Between life and death
Cautiously I peer into
The realms of possibilities
Dimensions separating
Salvation from suffering

A calming voice speaks
Death is but a doorway
Where one can find God
If one is worthy
Waking in a recovery bed
I realize I'm not yet worthy.

Dragonfly

Dragonfly dragonfly I can hear you sing
Travelling the realms with jewel encrusted wings.
Stopping to rest on a misty spring day
Soon to fly off and continue your play.

Darting in and out through the marshy grass
Chasing pixies over waters smooth as glass.
If ever you caught one what would you do
Force it to extend your life a month or two.

Stop your play long enough to propagate
Your enemies quietly lie in wait.
Attach your eggs at the edge of the marsh
Dropping them in water will be less harsh.

Now off you go to chase a pixie or two
I'm wishing I could go and chase them with you.
Dragonfly dragonfly I can hear you sing
Traveling the realms with jewel encrusted wings.

Easter Lily

Easter Lily, Easter Lily where were you conceived
In the Garden of Eden when Eve had to leave
Tears of repentance watered the ground
Where teardrops landed lilies were found

God's way of heralding in a changing age
Trumpeting Lily are you a silent sage
Resurrected each year in the spring
Like the lamb whose life forgiveness brings

Who's this man teaching forgiveness and love
Whose soul soars on the wings of a white dove
The blood of Jesus washed our sins away
It's He, who repented for us that day

Three days and Mary Magdalene did see
The resurrected Son that saved you and me
Easter Lily, Easter Lily let your trumpets sing
A reminder to us all that Christ is our King.

Easter Poem

A new day has started
He says welcome home my Son
The world is a better place
Because of all you've done

Relax now put your feet up
I've cooked a special treat
There are a few people
I'd really like you to meet

You gave them everything
That you could possibly give
The true believers have chosen
Where they want to live

On that Easter Sunday
You rose to walk away
An invitation was given
To come here to stay

So now the shepherd
Has brought his flock home
No more will those lost souls
Feel they're all alone

End Of Days

He stands in the shadows dressed in black
Once he's seen there's no turning back
With scythe in hand he harvests souls
To drag down to Hell's dank hole

He travels in the dark of night
Many souls don't put up a fight
But when his coffers run thin
He'll bring a pestilence in

The Reaper rides a pale horse
Death holds his reins of course
The fourth horseman comes this way
Heralding the end of days

 A great culling of the herd
Good and evil are all blurred
Some will perish under ground
Others will be heaven bound

A line in the sand has been drawn
Make your choice before time is gone
Jesus is your only way in
Only He can forgive your sins

Every Day Is Mental Illness Day

Sadness comes and the sadness goes
They try their best not to let it show
They live with the grief every single day
It cripples their life and won't go away

Some take medication to ease the pain
But the sadness comes again and again
Thoughts of aggression to ease the pain
Thoughts of self-destruction come again

The downward spiral comes and they hide away
Wanting it all to end, is what they pray
Pretending to be normal during their day to day
But late at night who dries the tears away

Calling in sick they can't face the day
It's a crippling illness that keeps them away
Silent cries for help fall on deaf ears once more
So they hide behind their closed locked doors

Then one night all their fears go away
An overdose of drugs earlier that day
This person has lost their fight
The world has lost another precious life.

ESCAPING THE DARKNESS: RUNNING FROM MY DREAMS

Fishing Town

Walking the shoreline as the fog rolls in
Puffy white clouds like alabaster skin
Waves breaking upon the jagged rocks
Sudden cold breezes across the docks

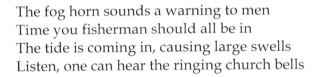

The lighthouse has lit up its light
The seagulls have all taken flight
Ten thousand candles lighting the way
A hot knife through fog many lives to save

The fog horn sounds a warning to men
Time you fisherman should all be in
The tide is coming in, causing large swells
Listen, one can hear the ringing church bells

Wives and families have met there to pray
Please god, our men and crews will you save
Guide them through the fog and reef tonight
Give them all the mariners' second sight

Just past midnight the last boat comes home
The church still full, no one was left alone
When those sailors opened the church door
They were met with a "Praise the Lord" roar

When the singing and prayers were all done
They walked outside to the rising sun
All survived and they are now worry free
Wives pray when their men go back to the sea.

A Day In The Desert (Haikus)

Morning dew brings life
Desert lilies are blooming
The sands grow hotter

A warm winter breeze
From across the desert plains
Smell the cactus flowers

Soon the dust will come
To cover us all in grit
Don't breathe too deeply

Slowly the sun drops
A beautiful orange sky
Stars twinkle all night

Heaven Bound

You have affronted me
Attacked me
Tried to knock me down
To rip my moral fiber
But I'm still standing

I'm still here
I do not fear you
You have no power
To control me
Push all that you will

And should I stumble
He will catch me
Support me
He is my protector
My guide

He walks beside me
Through the dark valley
Showing me the way
To the light beyond
For I am heaven bound.

I Am Merlin

Walking home one night I spied an eerie light
Was a burst of blueish flame which hurt my sight
Peering through the bushes seeing a man upon the ground
Another man was searching he was looking all around

Nearing death he spotted me I thought that I would die
Instead he slowly smiled pointing off to the side
The other man screaming curses filled me full of fear
Meanwhile the smiling one had turned a stone-deaf ear

Looking where he pointed I found an old black wand
As soon as I picked it up it formed a magical bond
The other man saw me and waved his wand at me
My wand sprang to life before I could think to flee

A blue light shot forth and full struck the other man
His wand burst into flames as it hurled from his hand
My wand hummed in mine as the old man faded away
A hundred years ago and I still remember that day

The day I saw the mage Merlin take his fatal fall
To that wand, that night I made myself to crawl
Two hundred years and Merlin lost his will to fight
I assumed his legacy, protector of the night

Seems an eternity since I fought my first fight
Burnt static in the air flashing lights in the night
The screams of demons I've sent back to hell
Am I winning this fight, only time will tell

Satan's minions coming after me because of Merlin's wand
I was chosen to wield that power with that magical bond
So now I battle sorcerers and demons of the night
I make them pay with the power of that fiery blue light

ESCAPING THE DARKNESS: RUNNING FROM MY DREAMS

I stand and fight for a world that lets the demons in
They don't understand it's caused from all their sin
This pitiful human race they haven't got a clue
I am Merlin. I alone, stand here protecting you.

Lady Of The Woods

Slowly she removes her veil
Her dress of white melting
She stands in the crisp morning air
Cool wet ground beneath her feet
Naked she lies down
On newly blossomed daffodils
She is the scent that floats
The beauty of the forest
The trees that give birth
The first buds of spring
She lingers on her bed
Listening to wood frogs
Awakened by her coming
They sing sweet lullabies
The forest awakens
She gives birth to the land
Sounds, smells, life
She is the Mother
She is the Lady of the Woods.

Let's Talk

I wake to another day
The sun shines outside
But inside my soul cries
Again my life has changed
Impending doom
I cannot function
My body and mind collapse
Inner turmoil rules the seconds
I scream silently for help
Wondering why no one hears
I'm praying for an end
Ready to walk away
From this life of torment
I hear banging at the door
But fear grips me
I am frozen in time
Instincts screaming to hide
Then you appear
Key in hand
You sit beside me
Saying nothing
Arms around me
Sobbing I turn to see
My true friend sitting with me
Together we share my tears.

Lines

I have drawn a line
In the sand
It represents my limits
A point that one cannot pass
A finishing point
But also a starting point
Should one simply stare
Beyond the lines confines
Looking for something
That can never be reached

Or simply turn around
Journey to the farthest point
Exploring life until
One reaches the line
On the far side
Lines are simply lines
A place to start
Or a place to end
The choice is yours
Choose wisely.

Listen

If I could only hear
The question you ask
Then I would answer
But how can I hear
When you don't speak
No hint from you
No sign from you
No time for you
I will walk away
Never to come back

Would you forsake me
Walk away from me
No
You would listen
But if not with my ears
Maybe with my heart
Ah I hear your voice
Ask of me
What you will
Lord.

Mirage

Tiny diamonds glisten
Sparkling on desert sand
The sun beats down
Creating shimmering waves

Watch as they dance
Before your eyes
Thoughts forming
In one's mind

Pictures appear
A cool oasis
Promising relief
From a relentless thirst

Immersed into the nightmare
Quick sand consumes
Swallowing slowly
Quenching its thirst.

Morning Prayer

An early morning sunrise
Beginning with a walk
Across serene sands
Ocean waves a serenade

To the coming day
A moment of pure solitude
In an otherwise hectic life
My time to commune

With God
And to see Him answer
In a beautiful smile
Of blazing colors

Promising forgiveness
Feeling contentment
I sit and gaze
Into the face of God.

My Friend

I have a friend who walks with me
Others question him; they do not see
This friend of mine never goes away
He's there to help me every day

I have a friend who walks with me
He doesn't charge he's totally free
He's there in sickness and in health
His presence with me is always felt

I have a friend who walks with me
In my darkest hour he hears my plea
I fear no evil while he is near
My cry for help he will always hear

I have a friend who walks with me
He died on a cross to set me free
He rose again to prove to me
His love for me will forever be

I have a friend who walks with me.

My Guide

I am never alone
Even in my darkest depths
He walks beside me
Guiding me through the darkness
Showing me the light
He tells me to look and I will see
Opening my heart, I see Him
In the warmth of the sun's embrace
I hear your promises in the air
Whispered through the trees
Birds singing your praises
The waters that bring life
You give me comfort
Protecting me from myself
You listen when others cannot hear
You are my friend, my confidant
I will follow wherever you lead
When it's time to go home
I go knowing thou art with me

My Happy Place

My secret place lies deep within
That special place where life begins
I find a spot upon the floor
No one around I've locked the door

Gently with head in hands
I search for serine ocean sands
One must try to clear their cluttered mind
Banish all the demons that they find

When Evil has nowhere else to hide
And fears are vanquished from deep inside
That's when I find my happy place
When God smiles down upon my face

I speak to God and He hears me
When kneeling on my bended knee
He knows already what troubles me
He cleanses my soul and sets me free

I ask, Lord what is it that I must to do
To join your table and sit with you
He shows a path made just for me
That I may live eternally.

My Journey

I was lost in the desert
An ocean of sand
For many days I traveled
Never knowing
If I would survive

Praying I asked
How long must I endure
What lesson
Are you teaching
I put my trust in you

On the seventh day
I came upon an oasis
Fresh water and fowl
I drank and ate
Filling my belly

Again I prayed
Thanking Him
For sending Providence
And He smiled
And spoke in a soft voice

I will send an angel
He shall guide you
Put you on the path
And lead you
Out of the wilderness

An angel appeared
Looking to the east
He spoke saying
Your destination awaits
I will guide you

I asked is this my path
To forgiveness
He replied to your salvation
Your journey begins
With your first step.

ESCAPING THE DARKNESS: RUNNING FROM MY DREAMS

New Beginnings

I lost the forward stabilizers and I knew I was about to die,
The Mother ship exploded like a fiery Fourth of July.
Like a surgeon's knife, the meteor cut through the forward bridge,
Snuffing out those precious lives like a fiery burning midge.

If only I can get to a pod I might escape this fiery fate,
I'll take my chances out there but first I must escape.
There's a small planet just off the port side,
I hope that I can make it, the pods on auto glide.

I landed on the deserted planet, glad to be alive,
Cautiously I opened the hatch to have a look outside.
A hazy looking atmosphere, a red sun is in the sky,
Steadying myself, I wondered what caused the locals all to die.

Might have been a nuke, more likely quite a few,
It left the air quite hazy with this morning's heavy foggy dew.
It's taken a thousand years, for life to grow up from the ground,
Plenty of mutated animals are roaming all around.

Could have been worse places for me to crash and die,
Suddenly I see another streak across that crimson sky.
The pod makes a rough landing and she comes crawling free,
I realize that she's the botanist; I think her name is Eve.

We come to realize that we alone survived that fiery fate,
Crashing on this little blue planet a thousand years too late.
Hello my name is Adam, I believe that yours is Eve,
Could be a long time till we're rescued; let's wait under this apple tree.

Petals

A rose captured in a vase
No more do its roots spread
It drinks its life dry
Until petals wilt
Slowly to wither and die

A marriage without love
Held together by a child
Loyalties divided
Wilted love corrupts
A child's vase runs dry

Pictures From My Mind

Vibrant colors of orange and red
Across an early morning sky
Feeling cool sand between my toes
The warm ocean water caresses me
Gulls soaring, screaming at the new sunrise
Sudden memories of brightly colored roosters
Heralding the new day
Squinting I see two souls holding hands
Wittiness's to the birth of the coming day
Staring at the now muted colors
My mind absorbing its essence
Trying desperately to take a mental picture
To create a high-resolution memory
I cry salted tears at a blue sky with wispy clouds
Light glistening off the receding tide
Sunlight fairies dancing across the waves
I see oysters squirting fountains on the beach
My mental camera captures each moment
God has given me another glorious day
Blind, but I can still feel the sun on my face
I watch the sunrise pictures from my mind.

Please, Please, I Want To Stay

Please, please, I want to stay
That is what I begin to say
Once again, He tells me that I must go
I'm not ready for that fantasy show

So here I lie in this hospital bed
I feel my pain; it's all in my head
The doctor tells me, "Hallucinations feel real"
But the chemo the drugs are all that I feel

I tell him, "I met a man there on the other side
He promised me that He'd be my guide
Through lush green lands, abundant with life
Free from pain and this miserable strife

It's a magical land with blue suns and colored clouds
A place where pain and grief is never allowed
Look! There's a unicorn laying just there
It seems to be talking to a long-eared hare"

The doctor tells me, "this is all drug induced"
While slowly he shakes his head, at the nurse
The pain increases I'm drifting away
Is this reality where I choose to stay

I hear the man calling, He that's my guide
Still waiting there for me on the other side
He tells me that if my pain is too great
He'll unlatch the lock and open the gate

All I need do is call his name
And forevermore I'll not feel pain
This cancer is real it's a disease I can't beat
I'm calling your name friend can I sit at your feet

ESCAPING THE DARKNESS: RUNNING FROM MY DREAMS

Please, please, Lord I want to stay
Please, please, Lord don't send me away
Here I lay my pain slips away
As I walk through that gate my body sways

Never again I'll not have to leave
My friend my guide, kept his promise to me.

Poets

The feelings I have today
The ones that won't go away
The ones that make my heart bleed
The ones I need you to read

They are what my soul needs to say
They are my living pain each day
They cry out for release
They only want to find peace

You are the only one you see
You can save me and set me free
You have all the answers I need
You can save a heart that bleeds

I know I'm not in a happy place
I can hide the grief upon my face
I slip in and out of reality
I am a poet setting my words free.

Prejudice

A different religion, a different race
Why do we say that we need our own space
We share the same ground, some sandy some loam
But at days dark end our roots call it home
We feel God's kiss in the warmth of the sun
The shiver of his breath when fall winds come
Come let our branches entwine and embrace
Let us find peace in God's loving grace
This is my hope, and my prayers
Let not our children live with despair
At the end of it all when our roots turn to dust
It is towards God, and in his love we must trust.

Rebirth

Yesterday's life has given way
To a new life born this very day
Let sorrows past remain where they lie
Allow bad memories to shrink and die
Remember the happiness, the joy, the sun
The light in your heart is from that one
Don't let the darkness control your life
Revel now in "Rebirth's" new light
For every darkness we must endure
Our love for the lost will always be pure.

Regret

Old man please tell me what do you see

I see nothing but pain and misery
I see children crying in the street
No medicine, no love, nothing to eat
I watch as many of them die
I squeeze tight my eyes and cry

Would be kings and conquers too
Famine and disease to me and you
A race for arms to see who will win
The war for humanity soon to begin

Old man please tell me what can we do

I fear nothing can be done for you
Maybe your children can save the day
Make this destruction go away
My life has been full of many regrets
Your children's children may save us yet.

Repent

Repent now before it's too late
Heaven has opened the pearly gates
Our time is nigh its judgment day
Will you go home or will you stay

Behold a scroll in God's right hand
Seven seals ruling all the land
The Lamb breaks four and all know fear
The first of the horseman soon appears

A rider on a white horse with bow and crown
The conquering king who will give no ground
Next a red horse, rider wielding a sword
No peace on earth just bands of warring hoards

A rider on a black horse with scales in hand
Bringing with him famine to all the land
The fourth horse was pale its rider is Death
Behind comes Hades to suck your last breath

The end starts, the horseman are here
Plagues and Hades' beasts bringing fear
The Antichrist laughs for he is now home
Laying waste to mankind, burning their bones

The dead have risen and are on their way
Disciples of false prophets kneel and pray
He's passing through like a thief in the night
The shepherd's flock already taken flight

I'm among his flock taken this night
Praying for those who suffer this plight
Praise be to God for saving this sinner
Everlasting life and my seat for dinner.

Ripples

I sit by the tepid waters
At the pool of memories
My fingers draw ripples
The water flows outward
Carrying ringlets of thought

On some astral plane
I remembered us
How our passion flowed
Like the waters in the pool
Hearts pounding with emotion

Galaxies explode in unison
The waters cool
Life is formed
Our universe lives
Man breathes

Suddenly through the darkness
Our minds touch
We linger for an eternity
Your interest intrigues me
I sense you reaching for me

For one fleeting moment
We coexist together
With a wave of my hand
A new ringlet forms
Memories ripple in the pool.

Salvation

The great lantern of the night
Has turned down its wick
The dawn approaches
Heralding a new birth

Morning birds awaken
Singing praises to the dawn
From the morning dew
Insects quench their thirst

Nature's nocturnals
Tamp down their beds
Away from prying eyes
The sun's warmth their blanket

As the moon bows
To the strength of the sun
Life begins anew
Growth through the light

Once more the circle
Is complete
From darkness comes light
From light salvation.

Saved

Most of my life I've hidden my pain
At times thinking I was quite insane
Two faces I carried around with me
Only one most people would ever see
The other a path to my personal hell
The place where evil and blackness dwell

Full of arrogance lust and vanity
Caring little for all of humanity
Still many nights I would kneel to pray
For help to keep my demons at bay

I feared there was nothing left for me
There lived no beauty inside to see
No more will I venture from these four walls
Nor will I answer when humanity calls
The mask I wore, the one people would see
Now lies broken on the floor before me

For a long time, I lived inside of me
The darkness would never set me free
Rock bottom. There was no other way
I planned my death for the very next day

When I awoke on that cold winter day
I saw a great ice storm had come my way
I ventured out but I couldn't believe
The greatest beauty that surrounded me
The sunlight was glistening in every tree
It seemed the world was sparkling just for me

CHRISTOPHER BICE

I sat on my steps for most of the day
Feeling that sunlight melt my fears away
I felt warmth inside of me
My heart, my soul, were now set free

I believed there was nothing left for me
Then God sent a message that I could see
I cried my first tears of joy that day
Realizing who took my darkness away
Knowing His love is what set my soul free
I feel His presence everywhere with me.

ESCAPING THE DARKNESS: RUNNING FROM MY DREAMS

<u>Searching</u>

Are we travelers
Moving through the universe
Or are we stationary
As the universe passes by us

If we could go faster
Than the speed of light
Would we end up at yesterday
Wondering about tomorrow

Why do we travel so far
Looking for God
Racing at the speed of light
But always ending up at the start

Why not just stop
Call His name
And He will come
Today yesterday and tomorrow.

CHRISTOPHER BICE

Second Chance

I awaken again it's been another restless night
This deformed old body has almost lost the fight
My whole life has been nothing but physical pain
People humiliate me. Pointing, I feel only shame
Treatments and surgeries left me crippled and weak
To most of this world I'm just some carnival freak

I dress and leave to walk the darkened streets
Avoiding hookers and lowlifes one tends to meet
My life has been harsh but I try not to complain
But I live a vicious cycle that's full of pain

Tonight seems different as I tread these lonely streets
There's an old lady pointing and she starts to speak
"I'm watching you closely and see your anguish and pain
Do as I say, I can make you feel alive again"
She tells me about a pool that she wants me to see
Refreshing waters that she promises will set me free

A hot humid evening maybe the water will feel good
A caring smile on her face as she motioned that I should
"At this point in your life you've nothing to lose
Remove all your clothing yes even your shoes"

I dip a toe and find the water amazingly warm
If it relieves some of my pain then what is the harm
Something in my head starts calling to me
"Immerse yourself old man, let me set you free"
Slipping deep into the waters I tremble with fear
But that soothing voice tells me I'm safe in here

Down deeper I sink and my body starts to glow
"Let go this old body and a new life I'll show"
I feel a tingling sensation as I let out my air

ESCAPING THE DARKNESS: RUNNING FROM MY DREAMS

Seems like an eternity that I'm suspended down there

Through my eyelids there's a piercing bright light
Squirming and gasping I'm losing this fight
I'm fighting for life, but think I'm dying
Grabbed by my feet, a slap, and I'm crying
That pool of forgiveness took away all of my strife
I awaken here, opening my eyes, to my new life.

The Brook

Babble babble you babbling brook
Chattering so loud I'll come to look
Tempting me to walk there
What will I see
Perhaps a flutter of water faeries
Kneeling low I hear them sing
Wondering what a new day brings
An errant step on a slippery stone
Next thing I know I'm wet to the bone
A trap was set and I fell in
I should have stayed where I had been
Laughing faeries all filled with joy
Almost drowned this poor little boy
White waters bubbling with glee
Yes little faeries you fooled me
Babble babble you babbling brook
I wish I'd never come to look.

ESCAPING THE DARKNESS: RUNNING FROM MY DREAMS

The Cowboy

The sun beats down on the sand filled plains,
It's dry cracked land that's ne'er seen rain.
A lonely cowboy rides with head held low,
His wide brimmed hat shading that burning glow.

The sun will dip beneath his feet,
The coming cold will hinder his sleep.
The torturous days of heat and thirst,
While horse and rider feel their worst.

Two more days of desert he must ride,
To reach the mountains on the westward side.
The battle emerges between sand and sun,
The cowboy has only one bullet in his gun.

His horse falters and misses its step,
The cowboy is feeling all his regrets.
Down falls the horse it cannot rise,
The lonely cowboy begins to cry.

One last bullet to end its pain,
The cowboy rises and begins again.
Does he make it to the end of the line,
Or simply vanish into time?

The Dolphin's Dance

The dolphins turn their rostrum high
Whilst gazing at the evening sky
Few understand their dancing at end of day
Chittering chattering together as they play
Racing each other then a leap through the air
The losers are clucking that it wasn't fair

They race towards the setting sun
Not wanting darkness to spoil the fun.
Just past the horizon is a brand-new day
Where they can meet again to jump and play

Poseidon looks up from his throne down below
Zeus looks down and tells the sun to hold its glow
Both are amused by the merriment they see
As these creatures pass through both realms wistfully
They cross over the horizon as day turns to night
So Zeus turns the earth so they can play in the light.

ESCAPING THE DARKNESS: RUNNING FROM MY DREAMS

<u>The Door</u>

In my sleep
I see the door
A massive oaken thing
On hinges of steel
I see the door
A massive oaken thing
On hinges of steel

The jambs are steel
Securing the door
In a free standing
Old growth grove

Slowly I walk
Around all sides
Seeing the door
From all directions

An old lift latch
With a single key way
Secures the door
Its bolt deeply embedded

There's a knocker
A hideous gargoyle
Watching quietly
Awaiting a brave hand

I try the latch
But it is locked
I knock three times
The gargoyle's voice echoes
Slowly the door opens
As I peer through

CHRISTOPHER BICE

Into the darkness
I see a small room

A chair sits facing
A large bookcase
Only one book remains
Covered in dust and mold

I pick up the book
Gently blowing the dust
From the canvas cover
Slowly I sit on the chair

The great oak door closes
As I read the book's title
'Secrets of a writer's mind'
I open it to chapter one.

ESCAPING THE DARKNESS: RUNNING FROM MY DREAMS

The Fog

Walk through the fog to a place of living dreams
Where Morla hides in muck fed by brackish streams
Ask not of him what dangers may lay ahead
If you want to live, then bypass him instead
If you encounter a pixie or a sprite
Better to run away than to stay and fight

Dangers are lurking hiding in the trees
A long day of walking to get clear of these
Soon you'll be through and on open ground
Stay wary of rock trolls they're all around

Bridges too have trolls, living underneath
Best to tiptoe across with just bare feet
If you can reach the plains on the westward side
Perhaps you can find an elf to be your guide
Bribe him to take you to the fairy queen
She can send you back to where you've been

A dangerous trip through the mountains for you
Losing sight of your elf you'll be a hapless fool
Dwarves in the mountains, Orcs on the roam
Either would flay all the flesh from your bones

Finally, in the valley where the fairies play
But meeting the queen will be a hundred days
You've lost your sanity reached the end of your rope
You tell the queen that you are doomed, there is no hope
With a wave of her wand, you realize you're back home
Finally realizing you've been to The Twilight Zone.

CHRISTOPHER BICE

The Hitchhiker

The tattooed hitchhiker arrived at the house
The man there was as quiet as a mouse
The man stood as the vintage clock chimed
I'm glad you made it at this somber time

Should we start now is what he said
I've got sick children to put to bed
The old man died a fortnight ago
You are the only one to show

This mysterious diary records voices you see
It's his last testament and he giggled with glee
Suddenly the crackly voice started so he sat again
"I leave all this to you but you must refrain"

"You may never wander the roads again
It's here you must live no matter the pain"
With her head shaking she started towards the door
I'm not staying here so I'll hear no more

Give the property and money to charity instead
Go home now and put your kids to bed
Proudly I'll hold my thumb in the air
I don't need this life; I'm more alive out there.

The Mountain

Once she had fire in her belly
A temper that spewed hot venom
But now she turns a cold shoulder
Her icy breath demanding respect
Blowing across translucent crevices
Threats from an unforgiving mistress
But now just painful memories
The sun glistens off slippery tears
Running down her face
Liquid misery falling below
Quenching thirsty basins
Deep pools of loss
Emerald green tears
Lakes steal her beauty
Waters reflect her lost splendor
A stark reminder of her sorrow
Naked she hides in despair
Veiled behind whispering clouds
Promising better days will come
She prays for a return to yesterday.

The Painter

The artist dips his brush

Careful not to drip the iridescent paint

Slowly the brush glides over living canvas

Strokes from a true master

Refractions spring to life

Blazes of colors alive and moving

Emotions running across the moonless sky

Vibrant colors changing with each stroke

Choosing a new mood from his easel

He slowly draws a line of pulsating beauty

Quietly he smiles at his creation.

The Path

I went searching
For enlightenment
Of why it is what it is
Over the mountains of despair
I crawled past the corpses
To ford the river of tears

Searching still
I feel the darkness reach out
The hysteria touch me
I fall to my knees
Sobbing uncontrollably

Then He touched me
With His knowing hands
He helped me rise
To see a path
Of how I could help

Where people help people
To see past the storm clouds
To a new dawn
When strangers become family
Compassion changes attitudes
And we all travel the path

To save humanity
We must look deep within
Until He touches us all
With His loving hand
To forgive others
We must first be forgiven.

CHRISTOPHER BICE

The Pear Tree

Too many drugs coursing inside of me
Hallucinations coming rapidly
Wrapping my blanket tight to me
I collapse under an old pear tree

Christmas Eve and I say my goodbyes
No family around to watch me die
I've hit rock bottom with nowhere to go
Don't it just figure, it's starting to snow

I start to shake uncontrollably
When suddenly a man speaks to me
I look up to see he's all dressed in white
His face is lit with a heavenly light

A miracle happened under that tree
This man of God gave my life back to me
The drugs oozed out from the pours of my skin
The Holy Spirit replaced the drugs within

The man looks at me with his smiling face
I was saved this night by God's good grace
He told me someone would come tonight
To lead me onto the path that's right

A heartbeat later and what did I see
A stranger soon came along to help me
I told him a miracle just happened to me
I was saved by a partridge in a pear tree.

ESCAPING THE DARKNESS: RUNNING FROM MY DREAMS

The Pool

They climb into the water

Slithering into their hot tubs

Noodles in the pool

The masses bobbing up and down

Chittering away

In blissful abandonment

Complaining

Too many chemicals

The waters are too cold

Turn up the heat

Gases and fluids seep

The tea is brewing

Steeped to perfection

Unsuspecting parents

Infectious births

Carriers

From the primordial ooze.

The Quill

I am but a vessel

I hold the ink

When He dips his quill

The words He writes

Become a part of me

His words shared through me

Onto the paper of life

So all may see and read His words

For all the glory is His

And His love is shared

Through the ink.

The Road To Salvation

For so many years
I traveled the road
Searching for something
I could not find

I approach a crossroads
Stopping to ponder
Which direction to take
I see Him, sitting

He simply says go east
But why I ask
It's your road to salvation
To forgiveness

He said I will walk with you
As your guide and protector
He offers His hand in friendship
Now my new journey begins

Years of searching now over
I now travel a new road
One to salvation and forgiveness
With my new best friend.

The Sands

I walk the wilderness
Across the sands of time
My tears salt water lakes
For eons I have searched
Lived millions of lives
Looking for the one thing
That has eluded me
Which I misplaced
While I traversed the deserts
My days consume me
The sun bakes me
The seemingly endless nights
As the moon cools me
Perhaps I've traveled too far
What I seek may be in the past
Looking back
I see the shifting sands
My path now obscured
Lost I fall to my knees
My time is done
Allowing my humanity to ebb
To become the sands
I find the lost thing
My soul.

ESCAPING THE DARKNESS: RUNNING FROM MY DREAMS

The Story Teller

The young boy approached the old man
He sat at his table head in hand
Excuse me sir said the young boy
Sheepishly holding his stuffed toy

Are you the story telling man
I'd love a story if you can
I love the way your stories rhyme
Could you tell one if you've the time

The old man lifted his head
He said to the lad go to bed
Tears in his eyes the lad walked away
The old man said wait, come back and stay

The lad ran back with a big smile
The old man says it's been a while
A moment please to find a starting place
The lad beamed with excitement on his face

The old man shed a tear from his eye
The lad asked are you going to cry
I've no stories left that are simply fun
Perhaps you could try to tell me one

The lad said this happened yesterday
I was in the ruins, that's where I play
Looking to see what I could find
When I saw this toy it blew my mind

The old man raised his hand to say
The ruins are full of death and decay
The boy laughed, nothing there to hurt me
The ghosts are long gone can't you see

CHRISTOPHER BICE

Going to the ruins and the things I see
The trip there through the beautiful valley
I see the grasses and valley flowers
Above lie the tumbled old rock towers
Smelling honeysuckles in the breeze
All entwined through the foresee trees
I feel the warmth of a summer sun
Promises of adventures to come

I never worry about the past
No more shadows will those dark days cast
The old man was wiping his eyes
The lad asked him why do you cry

I'm so happy we met today
Soon lad I must go away
I'll not worry who will take my place
It's you lad with that innocent face

People need story tellers don't you see
But I've no happy stories left in me
The past's dead and buried we are free
Please, tell another story to me

ESCAPING THE DARKNESS: RUNNING FROM MY DREAMS

The Thief

I walked into the coffee shop
To buy myself a brew
I spied him in the corner
I thought what has he been through

Asked the girl serving at the counter
What was this old guy's tale
Sadly she shook her head
Saying he maybe just got out of jail

That's when I decided
That this old man wouldn't sit alone
I bought him coffee and a doughnut
And invaded his comfort zone

Hey mister everyone has a story
And I bet you've got a tale to tell
And if you're not too busy
I'd love to talk with you a spell

Slowly he looked at me
With those old bleary eyes
He lowered his head slowly
That's when he starts to cry

The next couple of hours
I listened to what he said
I just couldn't believe
This old man was not dead

By the end of his story
It was I that shed a tear
I took his hand in mine
Said he had nothing more to fear

It was then he looked up at me
With eyes so bright and clear
Son I was looking just for you
You're the reason that I'm here

You passed this important test
You're one of the few
I've opened heaven's gates
We will all wait for you

Suddenly my heart burst open
Filled with a holy light
When I looked the old man was gone
Like a thief in the night.

The Veil

Slowly I draw back the veil
The darkness hides in shadows
I look beyond the obvious
Peering into infinity I see movement
Shadows lie in wait for careless travelers
Beyond the darkness I see a light
A beacon promising redemption, forgiveness
Reaching into the darkness I feel a rope
No, a tether
My heartstrings reach out for the light
In my mind I know to never let go
Fate is weaving my journey
Temptations pull at me
I see...
Possibilities
I feel the slow strum of a tune
Something playing at my strings
Surrender would be so easy
Come to me
Dance to the music
Live in the darkness
Drown in sinful pleasures
But the light still beckons
I can now feel the warmth
I reach for that curtain of light
My body glows with life
Forgiveness, is here
Suddenly I am surrounded
The lost have found me
I rejoice for I know I am home
I am filled with love
For He that guided me
Through the veils of death.

CHRISTOPHER BICE

What Goals Do We Have As Modern Man

What goals do we have as modern man
Simply to live the best that we can
At the end of the day who really cares
If our tree of life has fruit to bare

Will man remain on earth to grow
Will he survive here with anything to show
Catapulting to the heavens and stars
But do we really need to go that far

If our vanity and pride goes with us there
Years from now we'll still be living in despair
Is it better to lie in our unmade beds
Striving for unity and peace instead

Can we clean our waters, our air and land
Maybe it's here that we make our last stand
And if our trees truly have fruit to bare
Is it not our duty to show that we care

Yes its here that we plant our seedlings to grow
To them our legacy we will have to show
Nourish them with knowledge, compassion and love
Prove to them they needn't venture above

This little blue planet is theirs someday
As long as we haven't killed it along the way
So fertilize our ground so the seedlings will grow
And let our love of our planet be what we show.

Wordless

I awaken from another restless sleep
My mind has been pillaged and stripped of my words
I try desperately to form a coherent thought
I realize that you have plagiarized my meanings
Twisted my words
Looking into my soul, there is nothing there
You have already ripped it from me
I have laid it out for you on paper
I feel the ink from my pen drowning me
More words will come I just need to rest.

Words 1.0

I try to speak but nothing comes out
My tongue wraps about my eye teeth
I can't see what I'm saying
I murmur incoherent syllables
You are laughing once again
I feel like my words are bottled
Try as I might I can't speak to you
All these years and you still control me
I'm feeling trapped
I need to break free of you
Something must happen
I must regain my freedom
I need to break the bottle
Free my words
Use descriptive adjectives
Let loose my feelings
Speak for myself

Words 2.1

I listen to your explanation
Your words mean nothing
You twist the meanings
Discombobulating me
Trying to draw me in
Saying you love me
Whispered promises
Measured stanzas
A crescendo of lies
No more games
I see through you
Your words hold no power
Like your stories
They are full of holes.

Words 3.16

I stand here
Leaning against the podium
Trying desperately to speak
But I have no words
Something is missing
Taken from me
I feel a great loss
My throat clenches
I can't breathe
My vision blurs
Forcing tears of remorse
The page before me is blank
Rearrange the letters
Create new words
String them into sentences
I can feel my words
No longer full of holes
No longer disjointed
I can speak my thoughts
I can finally begin
"John," was a teacher
I learned much from him.

MADNESS

Apocalypse

I awake
To another hot morning
The sun shines red
Radiation boils uncovered skin
Atomic breezes that warm
Those hazy days of winter
I walk the wastelands now
Searching for survivors
But I fear I am the last
I cross over sands
Scorched so hot
They've been transformed
Into ruby lakes of glass
And the sun reflects death
After what seems an eternity
I see salvation in the distance
Silos from the last great nation
Cautiously I approach
To find one last sentinel
Rigidly standing guard
Dropping to my knees
I pray to God in heaven
But also to the tall silver God
Standing vigilantly before me
Its timer flashing reset
In my mind I remember
All that we were
What we became
And I find my answer
I push the button
I see the countdown
In the last few moments
Of man's last apocalypse
I smell brimstone

CHRISTOPHER BICE

I feel Hell's consuming fire
My last thoughts
Ashes to ashes
Dust to dust.

A Criminal Mind

I awake behind these cold hard bars
My life just one emotional scar
They're trying to keep me off the street
When I get out, they'll dance to my beat

I'm locked up in psychiatric care
But the doctors are getting no where
Drug injections all the time
Supposed to fix my broken mind

You see there was nothing wrong with me
My lawyer pled an insanity plea
Soon enough it'll be my turn
But for now, I'll watch and learn

For the guard I've planned a special trap
He'll be taking a permanent nap
Laundry company comes today
That's how I plan to get away

I'll find those twelve pitiful souls
The ones who put me in this hole
My committal papers they all signed
They'll soon die from a criminal mind.

CHRISTOPHER BICE

A Stranger In Town

The traveler walked in from the baking sun
His face told others not to mess with this one
Summer in this desert came with unbearable heat
Mid-afternoon and this man you didn't want to meet
A permanent darkness shone from those black eyes
Spontaneous combustion probably caused many to die

Vengeance has a price and he paid dear
Traveling those roadways all of these years
A scarred old map burned onto his skin
Pointing away from where he'd been

He asked questions of those from this town
Looking for the traffic patterns around
I think he needed a quick way to get away
For sure somebody was about to die this day
When he came to me those eyes cast a heat
My knees trembled his gaze I couldn't meet

He slid out the door and back into the heat
We peered out to see which way he went up the street
He turned into the alley again never to be seen
But we all heard the agonizing piercing screams

By the time the constables arrived it was too late
The man with those black eyes had already escaped
They tracked him to a farm outside of town
But battered bloody bodies was all they found
The town lived in fear for many a day
The stranger was already well on his way

Betrayal

When we met
I was a difficult mind
Wild unstructured
Your trust hard fought

I came to you broken
Praying you could help
I needed you to glue
My world together

You begged me
To let you in
To trust you
So I bared my soul

So many visits
Hours of appointments
A lifetime of pain
My tortured mind

Then betrayal
You pushed me away
Abandoned me
Institutionalized me

My mind collapsed
I fell into oblivion
Into a dark well
Of despair

Only to be recused
By something else
Now I listen to it
In my darkest madness.

Birth

First breath

Numbing cold

Terrifying light

Mind shattering panic

A soothing touch

First warm embrace

A Mother's love

Reprogramming contentment

My life begins

As a new recruit

For the human race

Another automaton

For the machine.

Destiny

I followed the path
Never to stray far
My destiny foretold
At birth

I am a soldier
Fighting for honor
But who's honor
I've never asked

The killing came easy
I was born to fight
But the hardest to kill
Are always the demons

Horrible ugly creatures
With the many faces
Of those I've ended
They haunt my dreams

I'm coming to the end
Honor holds no meaning
Too decrepit to continue
My honor stripped long ago

Soon I shall face my destiny
To ask if my true path
Was to unleash my madness
On an innocent world.

Disposable Person

I was near death
When I was found
I cried out in joy
Out of hunger
Out of loneliness

My sorrow had no bounds
Emotionally stunted
I matured slowly
Into a new age
Of disposable person

You gave me life
Then discarded me
Perhaps the way you
Were discarded by him
Mother and son alike

One almost died that day
One did die emotionally
Another disposable person
A disposable baby
Born in a dumpster home.

Dust

I lie on this cold slab
Leaving the same way, I came
What was once a birth swaddling
Now becomes a death shroud

I've just milliseconds left
Before my brain dies
Not much time is required
To relive this pittance of life

But there's never enough
To beg forgiveness
As my mind fades to black
I can feel the tug

My last curtain call
The last bow
As I slink out the back door
Elvis has left the building

My soul escapes
I soar upward to freedom
Just more dust in a universe
That never wanted me.

Extinction

As the new dawn approaches
I know this is my last sunrise
The crimson haze from the fallout
Creates an eerie veil
Of light and shadow
The air becomes heavy
Just before the coming rains

Humanity huddles in dank caves
The water that should bring life
Now burns the skin
A stark reminder of the end of days
Civilization fighting desperately
No healthy births these last few years
Extinction, just a matter of time

For me time has run out
No longer able to defend
My little square of shelter
The wolves will soon come
Man barely made the food chain
We are no longer the hunters
We are but cattle for wolves

I am the last reminder
Of a time before the cleansing
The blame is all on me
It is my fault that they suffer
My death may appease their gods
I pray my death brings salvation
It was I that pushed the button.

Genocide

Atop a boulder at the edge of the world
Flags of every country at my feet lie furled
The barrens before me dead and cleft
The end has come and what is left
As I'm gazing past all eternity
I dream a dream that I did not see

Civilizations ravaged turned to dust
All for would be gods and their power lust
I cry tears for the forgotten and lost
Wondering what has this genocide cost

It won't be long until I see
A last hazy sunrise for me
Sores on skin that do not bleed
A gift from false prophet's greed
Soon to succumb I will return to dust
Praying to God to forgive all of us.

__Hello__

Slowly he enters the room
Scanning the area to see
Who is worthy

At last, he sees her
The tall blonde
Sitting by herself

He works his way over
He comes up cautiously
Now in front of her

He approaches
Sliding in beside her
She looks at him and smiles

Her smile shows her fangs
She places her hand upon his leg
Hello is the last thing he remembers

Escaping the Darkness: Running from My Dreams

Hunter's Moon

The full moon evokes a low growl
The stench of rotting flesh too foul
Again darkness has consumed me
Everyone should really try to flee
The hunters will come this eve
Silver bullets made just for me

Final night of the hunter's moon
When lovers entwined still swoon
Too entranced to hear my mournful cry
Or to noticed my pale-yellow eyes

It's too late for them you see
Their bloody gore is all over me
Their screams still linger in my ears
Hunters shouting coming near
From Cerberus I was spawned
Fast as I came now, I'm gone

When the new dawn comes so I'll change
Fur falling from me like diseased mange
Crawling to hide deep in my hole
Praying for God to save my soul

For another month I'll be human again
Until Cerberus calls me back to this plane
He demands vengeful homage from me
It's the price that I pay to live free
Keep close watch over your families
The last evil you will see…is me.

Insanity

Why do they hunt me what harm have I done? I stay to myself unless you invite me to come. If you don't want me then you should have stayed inside. I love hide and seek so best you run and hide. Pray that you win and I don't find you...there's no telling what I may do.

You call me crazy
But that can't be
I just crossed a line
And found the real me
A sinister thing inside
That was trapped
It clawed its way free
When my mind snapped
So it's my turn to run
And you'll never find me
I play hopscotch with the line
Between genius and insanity

For now, this genius will run away. Maybe I'll come back someday to play. Until then hold dearly your children, your husband, your wife. If my insanity breaks free I'll end their life. But before I have to run away again. Let's play one more game... I'll count to ten.

Killing My Demons

I'm living in a nightmare
One I can't control
The dampness on my pillow
Comes from my crying soul

My whole tortured being
Screaming for release
Demons that bind me
Know I'll not find inner peace

So how do I end this nightmare
How do I break free
Do I give in to the demons
See if they let me be

Maybe a killing rampage
Is exactly what I need
Perhaps a bloodletting
Could it be me, that needs to bleed

Both answers seem most likely
So, I'll try both out tonight
First, I'll send sacrifices
Then bloodletting at daylight.

Lessons Learned

No one knows
All the pain
I've been through

All the lessons taught
From the hands
Of you

I was just a defenseless
Child growing up
In fear

Cringing every time
You came home
Drunk from too much beer

I learned my lessons well
How to turn
The other cheek

But no longer
Am I child
Defenseless and weak

Time to end
The beatings
When you get bored

No more will
I suffer
You'll be in the morgue.

Lonely Street

I travel down the lonely streets
Staying away from those I meet
Finding a bench, I sleep alone
The back alleys are now my home

The deadline is approaching
Preaches the zealot who's coaching
He always tries to convert me
I live on the streets but I'm free

I search for things that I can swap
To make enough for the coffee shop
Sometimes I get the owner's spouse
Who gives me a coffee on the house

I'm not wealthy but I am rich
Single and free no one to bitch
If you ever come down to lonely street
I'm not the beggar that you want to meet.

Love's Feast

Come to me my lovely
Fall into my arms
Let me seduce you
Using all of my charms
Running my fingers through your hair
Whisper sweet nothings in an ear
All the while my roaming hands
Saying you've nothing to fear
Your lips slowly start to open
Inviting the tip of my tongue
My hands have found the clasp
Your bodice soon to be undone

You pop the buttons off my shirt
I feel it start to rip
You run your fingers across my chest
With soft finger tips
You can't believe you're doing this
As you begin to swoon
Your bleary gaze moves around
To the bed across the room
Hot breath causing tingles
As my teeth sink to the bone
Deception my lovely
But vampires always eat alone.

Lover's Kiss

I sit in darkness
Brooding
The night as black
As my soul

Slowly I sink
Into the deepest depths
Of despair
Realizing suddenly

That death is my lover
That sorrow is
A lover's kiss
Turning a heart cold

As cold as the night
Still my lover calls me
Come to me
Come lie forever

Within the arms
Of your dead lover
Inside a mind lost
To the night's insanity.

Memories

Sometimes I wonder
If I've already lived my life

If the works I've written have
Already been written before

Am I just plagiarizing
Copying words from the past

Are my words
Somebody else's life

Am I writing in first person
Or from the lives of the many

If so then who were they
And what does that make me

A scoundrel or just a thief
A second-rate poet

Perhaps my body holds
Old souls that guide my pen

If so then when I'm gone
Who will write my words

Will anyone read our lives
On tear-stained papers

With the quill dipped
Into the souls of the many.

Multiples

I look at you and I see me
But agony lies within my arm
Roadways to a dead end
I need more to keep going
You are my dead end
Closing my eyes, I feel pain

Slowly I open my eyes
Afraid of everything I see
My mind cries out in fear
I'm trapped in here with them
Quickly I close my eyes again
Squeezing my fears away

Now I show you my anger
Can you see me for who I am
I am destruction I am death
Set me free to rule the night
I will murder you all
As you sleep in your beds

Waking I find you still here
I ask if you found the one
You simply tell me no
I must regress once more
I trust you doctor...but
How many are we?

My Magic Phone

I have a magic phone
It's a lovely shade of red
I love my magic phone
It sits here beside my bed

When I'm feeling sad
And from this room I cannot roam
I dial up my Mother
To talk with her at home

Sometimes my sister answers
To say that Moms gone away
But it's okay my baby brother
Let's have some fun and play

I say that I wish I could
But the men are coming back
They wear those white coats
And connect me to electric jacks

I can't take the shocks
That they send through my head
Sister, please tell Mom
I wish that I was dead

Oh, sister I have to go
Have to hang up my magic phone
It's okay little brother
Today you'll be coming home

So, go with the men
Please try not to be afraid
I'll watch for your arrival
We've planned a big parade.

New Year

It's a new day
Of a new week
Yes, a new month

Hesitating beyond the walls
Of her concrete prison
She slowly walks away

Self defense
At last free from pain
Free to live

Free to heal
Her broken heart
Her damaged soul

Vowing never to go back
A promise made
From the heart

It's my turn she thinks
I am in control
To choose my path

She feels the sudden rage
The blackness within
Her all-consuming hatred

I will be the master
They will all suffer
In this New Year.

Pandemic

Butterflies trapped

Locked in the stomach

Throat convulsing

Weakness

Behind the knees

Short shallow breaths

Drowning in uneasiness

The dreaded shakes

Urges to stockpile

Solitary confinement

Panic attacking

A global pandemic

Not of disease

But of FEAR.

Escaping the Darkness: Running from my Dreams

Retribution

He came from the sewers
Where the demons were fewer
They didn't like the flies
Always landing in their eyes

He crawled through the long sage grass
The blades cutting his skin like glass
Years of dank living underground
Made the lesions on his skin profound

But pixies and fairies in the garden
May take mercy and give him a pardon
Heal his body and soul
Once again he'd be whole

So now he walks like a man
And he comes up with a plan
He walks across the ocean sand
A pixie held inside his hand

That night they fell in love on the beach
The pixie in question stayed within reach
Together they planned a new life
No more demons or cursed nights

For pixies, love can never be claimed
She suddenly burst into blue flames
He cried the accident wasn't my fault
To Pixies excuses are just grains of salt

Transformed back no longer a man
Slowly he crawls back from the sands
Back down into the sewers he fell
To demons and his own little hell.

Shattered

I walk through the door
Footsteps echoing my emptiness
I see the tree lights are on
The unwrapped presents
Still lying on the floor untouched

It's Christmas Day
And I've lost the fight
The Greyhound left at five a.m.
The kids crying as they board
Me crying as my world shatters

I look again at the Christmas tree
My anger no longer controlled
It lands on the sidewalk
The ornaments exploding on impact
My heart mirrors the fragmented glass

Quietly I close the door
I stack the gifts neatly in a closet
Living my pain, I take all the pills
I go to bed to cry myself to death
Sadly, I awake two days later.

Shipwreck

Blowing wind with deafening hail
Breezes turning to a deadly gale
Batten the hatches the captain cried
Quickly mates or we all will die

The sun blocked it was black as night
They were in for one helluva fight
Praying to Poseidon, the other gods too
Thinking today they will pay the Devil his due

Lightening striking midway on the mast
Everyone knew this day was their last
The boat was listing it wouldn't be long
Until every last sailor would soon be gone.

To the lifeboats the captain said
Hop to it lads or we'll all be dead
The ship went down on that fateful day
Lost all their gold but the Devil was paid

The storm blew out later that day
Now the tides must carry them away
Land ho; I think I can see the shore
Figures he mutters Bermuda's front door.

Tears Of The Damned

I walk the shoreline
Along an ocean of tears
Looking for a life jacket
Or a lifeboat
Anything to keep me afloat

But the quicksand beach
Draws me deeper
Closer to the lapping waters
I open my mouth to scream
But tears drown my cries

The sands of time
And the ocean of tears
My existence washing away
Like I was never born
Never a memory

As the tides recede
So too do my dreams
Drowning in the deep eddies
I give in to the swirling waters
And forfeit all hope

My body lies motionless
Death my release from pain
Tears of the damned
Running down my cheeks
Dreading an eternity of loneliness.

ESCAPING THE DARKNESS: RUNNING FROM MY DREAMS

The Banshee

In the pubs he'd tell his tales,
Of how life changed when he furled his sails.
All his life he spent on the seas,
That's where he'd heard stories of wild Banshee.

He'd heard the stories of Banshees, up in the hills,
That's where old sailors' fears are fulfilled.
Now in the pubs he tells his tales,
Of terrible Banshees and their fearful wails.

Walking at night he ventures home,
He's walking the hills, he's all alone.
Finally, at home, he quickly tries his key,
Still fearing the tails, of the old Banshee.

Tripping over the sill he ends up on the ground,
Looking up the stairs, the Banshee stares down.
He hears that fearful scream,
He's wishing that it's just a dream.

The hairs on his neck have started to rise,
All he can see are those murderous eyes.
She flies down the stairs and begins the attack,
He has no way of fighting back.

Something is swinging; it pounds his head,
His last thoughts are of dying, he believes he is dead.
When morning arrives and he's survived the night,
There's no longer a Banshee anywhere in sight.

He sees his wife descending the stair,
Something in her eyes appears familiar there.
All the stories he tells, could they be true,
Is there a Banshee living at home with you?

Tell your Wife you'll give up the drink,
And this tall tale will end with her knowing wink.

The Birth Of Madness

A child is born
Into a family torn asunder
Ripped apart at their core

Growing up lost
Living his pain
Fearing his life

His emotions
Held tightly to his chest
Hidden in the darkness

Nurturing his anger
Strengthening his resolve
Clouding his mind

He feels nothing
His hatred explodes
The evil expels

Thus, is the birth
Of a new age
Of madness.

The Book

I was on the prowl for something a bit more
I found it in the second hand book store
I was looking when off the shelf it fell
A leather book of rare old magic spells

I asked at the desk if it was for sale
Oh she said, 'that book has a few tales
Its got a good story or two
But I don't think it's for you'

Old crone standing there grinning
She lied from the beginning
The price, it was a crime
But now that book is mine

My friends were waiting so I didn't walk far
I jumped in the backseat of their old car
Slowly I unlatched the gold lock
And that's when things got really hot

But that's another tale to tell
One more suited for when I'm...well
For now be content when I say
I found more than a book that day.

ESCAPING THE DARKNESS: RUNNING FROM MY DREAMS

The Breakdown

I wake to another mundane day
The morning sunbeam dries my eyes
The lonely day awaits my company
Together we stretch our silence
City streets of deafening chaos
Throngs of conceit and anger
Walking around me, past me, through me
Sitting in an outdoor patio
Watching as life passes by me
Waiters and patrons oblivious to me
Leaving, my water glass still empty
My heart now heavy with despair
My mind is a void of nothingness
Am I even here
Can you see me
Do I even exist
My soul screams for recognition
People continue past me unaware
My mind realizes I am not here
I fall into the well of madness
Curling up I drown in anguish
My mind breaks and I feel nothing
I am consumed by the darkness
Lost, unreachable, unloved
I am alone.

The Dungeon Master

I prefer dark places out of the light
I drool a little when they put up a fight
My job is to torture and maim
My employer is quite insane

He rules above out in the light
I rule the dungeon dark as night
Enemies of the state come here to stay
I giggle because it's my time to play

My Master pays me to inflict this pain
But I'd do it for free again and again
I'll straighten out your back
With a few twists on the rack

With my red-hot iron just out of the fire
Caressing your legs, your screams go higher
You'll wiggle and squirm and try to fight
Your screams fill me so full of delight

White hot pokers to sear out your eyes
I get so excited just hearing your cries
My Iron Maiden with few hundred nails
Will bleed you slowly as they impale

I'm sorry to see that you weren't so strong
You bled straight out and now you're gone
Pre-dawn's light is showing soon to be day
I'll wait for darkness and another to play.

ESCAPING THE DARKNESS: RUNNING FROM MY DREAMS

The Evil Within

I've been forced to travel many lands. Because of what I held in my hands. Something in a pyramid buried deep. Something so evil that I dare not speak. The lid somehow came off in my hand. A smoke-filled vessel full of black sand.

Since that night on the pyramid floor
My life is full of mayhem and gore
That evil was from an ancient land
Sealed inside until touching my hand

Soon after that I started to change
The evil inside me felt quite strange
The next thing I knew I had to flee
The bodies were piling up around me

From Jordan to Cairo into Sudan
The evil inside seems to have a plan
Into the desert there's nothing but sand
Topping a dune, I finally see its plan

A pyramid half buried underground
I dug until a doorway was found
I feel my bile starting to rise
Inside were dead alien guys

I felt the evil setting me free
As it transferred over to it from me
The alien started gasping for air
I thought it best to get out of there

The ship started humming coming to life
It sliced through that pyramid like a knife
It burst forth then darted away
I dropped to my knees and prayed

My picture's all over the TV. The police soon caught up to me. When that black evil left it abandoned me. No one believed me so I plead insanity. So here I'm trapped an innocent man. Because of an evil that invaded my hand.

ESCAPING THE DARKNESS: RUNNING FROM MY DREAMS

The Grim Reaper

Walking home last evening it was a terrible night,
My wife and I had us a wicked mean fight.
I stormed out the door and was in a drinking mood,
Down to Murphy's Tavern I go so I could brood.

I poured back the scotch without any food,
The more I drank the fouler my mood.
Out the door Murphy threw me and said, go home,
His dog growled at me; I screamed leave me alone!

I staggered to the cemetery; it's a shortcut home,
When suddenly I felt like I was not alone.
Something moved in the shadows, I stopped to stare,
The hairs on my neck told me to say a prayer.

I knew it was the Grim Reaper he was coming for me,
Suddenly I got sick, I fell to my knees.
I begged I could change, it was my drunken plea,
You stupid drunkard. I'm the gardener out for a pee.

It pains me to tell you this but I woke up in bed,
My stomach wrenching from the massive pain in my head.
I told my wife I was sorry about the fight,
You know I told her, I almost died last night.

So here I am now contemplating my new life,
The Reaper spared me and brought me home to my wife.

The Madness

I feel the madness deep within
That thing inside me slowly grins
The darkness comes once again
My stomach wrenches with the pain

Slowly it takes control over me
I hide within nowhere to flee
It forces me to inflict pain
Please help me I'm going insane

A knife appears from out of thin air
I cut my wrists with no time to spare
Needing to bleed this madness from me
It's the only way I'll be free

I scream at the sight of my own gore
The madness is floating on the floor
A calmness soon comes over me
I think finally, I'll be free

I drift off knowing I'll soon be dead
But I wake up in a hospital bed
A transfusion line connected to me
Restores more madness I'll never be free

They have a special room just for me
Where the madness will let me be
Doctors talk to me every day
But my madness won't go away

There's only one way I'll be free
One way to take this madness from me
But first I must play their stupid game
Then bleed it out before I go insane.

ESCAPING THE DARKNESS: RUNNING FROM MY DREAMS

The Scale

I avoid the cobblestone roads staying mostly on dirt paths. Wizards are not welcome on the roadways with the mundane. We are scorned and feared unless of course one has need of us, then when the problem is fixed, we are shunned again.

I walk the shadow paths
Just beyond reach
Of the sun
Of light
Of the people
Of life

When needed they find me
At dusk when the sun dies
Falling to its grave beneath the horizon
When the moon controls the world
When their demons come
I am summoned

They fear it, more than me
But am I not the greater evil
If I can kill their greatest fears
Then are their lives
Not just a snap of my fingers
They are just the pawns

I am the ruler of the night
No stallion do I ride
My subjects crawl to me
Begging for my mercies
I show them salvation
As long as payment is made

I walk the path between good and evil, the darkness and the light. I am the scale that balances two worlds. My magic may be bought to tip those scales, in one's favor. Who needs me tonight and what price are you willing to pay?

The Seventh Son

It's been nigh onto two-hundred year
Since your evil ways were last seen here
Your imprisonment was to curtail your charms
Locked beneath the ground you could do no harm

The gate is now weathered and very old
You know that shortly it will not hold
Soon to be free the terrors would begin
Everyone would pay for that heinous sin

You test the runes on that magical gate
Once they are breached mankind is too late
A blood moon is coming within a fortnight
It'll be too late for mankind to put up a fight

I'm not totally human I carry mixed blood
Spawned from a witch and human that fell in love
I was born when the sun turned black at mid-day
Body crackling with magic, I'll not run away

So send your minions to chase after me
I'll send them back to Hell, I will not flee
When you do finally escape and break free
I will make it real easy for you to find me

Perched on this hilltop I'll be easy to see
Bring yourself here. This fights between you and me
You will soon find that I'm not to be riled
The air will sizzle with magic gone wild

I'm the seventh son
Of a seventh son
And no mercy to you, will I show
Till you're buried deep, back in your hole.

The Tower

There's a black tower that beckons to me
But it's not a structure that you can see
It lies hidden deep within my mind
It's not something you'll want to find

This tower holds all my blackness in
Prevents me from doing evil sins
Should the blackness ever break free
It would be best to run from me

I've had doctors and shrinks try to get in
Peer through a crack then close the door again
Shock treatments to try and make me sane
But the blackness lives off of the pain

Fools think they can rehabilitate me
When the tower door opens, they will see
A weakened door soon to be unhinged
Then mortal men will bow and cringe

Government cutbacks have set me free
There's nothing now keeping you from me
With my darkness free to roam the night
Pray you can hide and stay out of sight.

The Wilderness

I walk through a wilderness

Unable to get my bearings

Lost and forgotten

Trapped like many souls

Unable to find their way

Forcible confinement

Slave labor

To corporate overlords

Work camps

Living a slow death

An automaton of civilization

Taking a lifetime to break free

Your pittance of freedom

From the concrete jungle

Escaping just in time to succumb.

The Wizard

Last night I met a wizard
He lives up on the hill
He said he knew my troubles
And he fixed them with magic pills

And the stars upon his cape
Glowed brightly in the evening sky
My worries seemed to float away
With a feeling that I could fly

And when the night was done
And the dawn came sneaking in
The wizard had flown away
I had no idea where I'd been

My problems now feel so small
After my enlightenment last night
I see things so differently now
The wizard gave me second sight

So should your problems get you down
And you think you're drowning in your bills
Then come my friend and seek me out
The wizard gave me the magic pills.

Unbelievers

I open my eyes
To find I'm lying on the floor
I rise to see many people
Or possibly shades of people
Standing, waiting, for what
I'm in a vast area
Of pure white
The starkness overpowers me
The silence is deafening
I look around me in all directions
The throngs slowly crushing me
No room to breathe
I feel pain inside me
Suddenly I see a shimmer
I reach for it and there is a door
In my ear a slight breeze
As I open it, I hear a whisper
They are unbelievers
They will not listen
The pain comes again
A bright light
Hurting my eyes
Gasping for air
Colors explode
A detached voice
Exclaiming he's back
A whisper in my ear
Unbelievers.

Untitled Unfinished

I awaken with the realization that

I survived another hellish night

Alive but not unscathed

My nightmares torment me

Following my every move

Criticizing me

Cutting me to the bone

A thousand tiny cuts

My success, my inspiration

My soul, ooze from those wounds

I dip my quill in my own gore

Desperate to capture my thoughts

But alas the well has run dry

The parchment turned to dust

I'm left speechless

I now understand my nightmare

I must leave my dreams behind

ESCAPING THE DARKNESS: RUNNING FROM MY DREAMS

Explore new paths

Search for inspiration elsewhere

Walk away.

Working Man

I wander through the wilderness
Wanting to leave my mark
But every tree I touch turns
As I glance behind me
My marks are gone
Erased from sight
My history changed forever
I no longer know where I came from
Every path another dead end
It starts to rain
Sympathetic fallacy
From a wilderness without feelings
Full of hidden agendas
Self-preservation
Survival of the fittest
I feel my strength draining
Slowly I succumb
Losing myself
To the madness
An automaton
A mindless slave
To an unforgiving city.

ABOUT THE POET

Christopher Bice grew up in Brantford, Ontario, and moved West with his family to a small village in Northern BC.

After many years he returned to the East and met his wife. They later came to Coalhurst Alberta (just outside of Lethbridge) to retire. Other than writing, Christopher enjoys fishing and camping and finds his inspiration while out in nature.

Manufactured by Amazon.ca
Bolton, ON